THE JEWISH MUSEUM
OF BUDAPEST

THE JEWISH MUSEUM
OF BUDAPEST

ILONA BENOSCHOFSKY
AND ALEXANDER SCHEIBER

editors

Translated from the Hungarian by
Joseph W. Wiesenberg

Corvina

Title of the Hungarian original :
A budapesti Zsidó Múzeum, Corvina Kiadó, Budapest, 1987

Written by
Ilona Benoschofsky, Alexander Scheiber,
Ilona P. Brestyánszky, Katalin F. Dózsa, Dénes Deák,
Photographs by László Szelényi
Jacket by Miklós Kozma

CONTENTS

THE HISTORY OF THE MUSEUM

In 1896, Hungary celebrated her millennium by organizing a great exhibition. At this exhibition, the Churches introduced their artifacts. The Jewish community was represented by ninety pieces. Though this number is praiseworthy, the exhibited articles were rather poor. There were no truly antique pieces among them and those that were exhibited as such could not pass close scrutiny. Few were also the artistic exhibits. One of the reports on the exhibition[1] deals at length with the question of why Jews have no genuinely antique and artistic ritual objects. The Biblical command, "You shall make no graven images," has been misunderstood for centuries by Jews of the Middle Ages and modern times, thereby hindering the development of Jewish art. Indeed, they made no "graven images", neither statues, nor portraits. Furthermore, even those old congregations in Hungary whose history can be traced back for many hundreds of years ceased functioning from time to time during Jewish persecutions; their synagogues were destroyed, and their ritual objects disappeared.

Both congregations and private individuals had sent material to the Millennial Exhibition. However, the organizers—for reasons unknown—exhibited the inferior exemplars and rejected the superior items. Still, a few significant items were included, such as the manuscript of Izsák Schulhof who had been present at the liberation of Buda from the Turks and, in his memoirs, described the battles as they took place, the fate of Buda's Jews, and his own.[2] But the majority of the material, in form and in execution, was almost primitive.

Another report of the Exhibition[3] also stresses that there are few hundred-year-old ritual objects in Hungary not only because the old synagogues had been destroyed, but their equipment—according to the author—had been rudimentary to begin with. On one occasion, before the Millennial Exhibition, the general public could have seen Jewish ritual objects at the National Historical Silverware Exhibition of 1884. It seems, however, that this very early first Jewish exhibition received less attention than the exhibition of 1896. From the point of view of our Museum, the Jewish material of the Millennial Exhibition, though ever so primitive, has a very important and significant role. The author of the second report was Miksa Szabolcsi, the editor of *Egyenlőség* (Equality), the popular weekly. The plan of establishing a Jewish museum occurs to Szabolcsi in connection with the Millennial Exhibition. The thought comes to him that everything exhibited and everything rejected in the Exhibition ought to be kept together. "However poor we are in data referring to the past, the exhibited and not exhibited but submitted material *together* contains invaluable material on our history. The interesting and valuable part: manuscripts, documents, books were scattered far and wide before they could be collected, and all that did get shown will also be scattered in a few weeks—and we are so very poor in historical data! *Perhaps we could keep the things that are together and enrich them with those that did not get selected for the Exhibition.*" Further, even more concretely: "Let us create a storehouse of Jewish collections whose foundation would be the exhibited and rejected (we repeat: these are the more valuable) articles and it will be the responsibility of the future to enrich it and make it famous."

Further in his report, Szabolcsi is confident that "not a few locked cabinets which hold valuable Jewish antiques not sent to the Exhibition will be opened to pass them on willingly to the Jewish Museum".[4]

This is where Szabolcsi first mentions the idea and plan of a Jewish Museum to be founded in Budapest. Many people reacted to the article with eagerness. Of these, the most important was Sándor Büchler's article.[5] "No doubt," he writes, "the Jewish Museum would be a most welcome institution whose value would lie not only in illustrating the history of Hungarian Jews with the exhibited objects, but chiefly, it would serve the important purpose of *awakening a sense of history in Hungarian Jewry.*"

Büchler continues to relate how so many important valuables of Hungarian Jewry are ruined. Old and rare gravestones are used to build cemetery fences; important documents of congregations land on the shelves of general stores; masterpieces of synagogue silversmiths go to ruin in tiny rural congregations, and there is not a single congregation in the entire country with organized archives. He sees as the most important objective of the future Jewish Museum to awaken the interest of congregations and individuals in the past of the Jews of Hungary, and to start them collecting, guarding and cherishing their values.

He also speaks about the Óbuda congregational archives that preserves the congregation's history from the end of the eighteenth century to the middle of the nineteenth. If the congregation were to transfer this invaluable source to the Jewish Museum, this would, without a doubt, encourage other congregations to do likewise.

The two articles, that of Miksa Szabolcsi encouraging mainly the gathering and showing of religious objects and that of Sándor Büchler advising the collection and exhibition of sources, i.e., historical documents, were influential in forming a plan to found a Hungarian Jewish religious and historical museum. Though we have no documentary evidence for this, it is certain that the plan had been present in Jewish consciousness—so much so that when the most important cultural organization of Hungarian Jewry, the Hungarian Israelite Literary Society (Izraelita Magyar Irodalmi Társulat—IMIT)[6] had its session in December 1909, the collection of artifacts had already started. At this session, Dr. Ferenc Mezey, secretary of the Jewish community's most prominent organization, the Central Board of Hungarian Jews (Magyar Izraeliták Országos Irodája), moved the following: "Whereas, the collection and exhibition of objects relating to the history of the Jewish people, their spiritual life, religious culture, tradition and artistic genius such as ritual objects, superior old artifacts, portraits, silverware and documents are not only of sectarian but of *general* artistic and cultural interest and, whereas, the establishment of such collection reflecting our country's Jewish religious life would also be of extreme significance from the perspective of national education, and considering the fact that the desire for such a collection is evident in our religious community, for some individuals have already begun work on such a project with great understanding; more, since the idea has met with approval and a readiness to sacrifice among our intellectuals, the time for positive action has come. Be it, therefore, resolved that the Hungarian Israelite Literary Society extends its activities in this direction and establishes a Jewish Museum and, to this end, a separate foundation is called into being; it further creates a Special Commission to manage the project and resolves at the same time that the by-laws of this Commission shall be completed satisfactorily at the next general assembly."[7]

The motion was passed by the directors of HILS (IMIT), who decided to set up a Museum Commission. The chairman of the Commission was Ferenc Székely, bank director, prominent personality of Jewish cultural life; his co-chairman was the person who had made the motion, Dr. Ferenc Mezey. Members of the Commission were: Bernát Alexander, philosopher and aesthete, university professor; Vilmos Bacher, orientalist, professor at the National Rabbinical Seminary, later its director; József Bánóczi, philosopher and literary historian, professor at the University of Budapest, corresponding member of the Hungarian Academy of Sciences, director of the Israelite Teachers' Training Institute;

Jewish gravestone from the 3rd century. Site where found: Esztergom. Limestone. 75 × 43 cm. Inventory No.: 64.1963

Lajos Blau, Talmudist, professor at the National Rabbinical Seminary and after Bacher's death its director; Bertalan Fabó, music historian, researcher of old Hungarian music, later the Museum's first curator and one of the editors of the Museum's catalogue; Adolf Fényes, painter; József Keszler, aesthete and critic, journalist, French language and literature professor of the Budapest Teachers' Training Institute; Bertalan Kohlbach, rabbi, high school teacher, contributor to many learned journals; Adolf Kohner, landowner and industrialist, President of the Central Board of Hungarian Jews, art collector; Béla Lajta, architect; Ede Mahler, Assyrologist–Egyptologist, university professor; Bernát Mandl, pedagogue and historian, researcher of Hungarian Jewish history; Henrik Marczali, historian, university professor, member of the Hungarian Academy of Sciences; Mór Spitzer, district chairman; Mór Stiller, jurist, editor; Béla Surányi; Miksa Szabolcsi, author, editor, one among those who disproved the Tiszaeszlár blood-libel; Ede Telcs, sculptor; Lajos Venetianer, Chief Rabbi, historian, professor at the National Rabbinical Seminary.[8]

It was not only the high intellectual caliber of the Commission that was important, but also the fact that the majority of those elected to it took their appointment very seriously. They worked on the establishment and enhancement of the Museum with utmost dedication and diligence.

Hardly had a few days passed when the Commission had already presented a motion to the Board of the Hungarian Israelite Literary Society, in which they defined the task ahead in part as follows: "When we suggested planning a national Jewish museum and set the project on the path of realization, we did that in response to the Society's leadership. We wish to collect and preserve the memorabilia of our national religious life, the scattered witnesses of our historical struggles and intellectual movements in order to demonstrate the creative talent of the Jewish soul in the past, to stimulate it in the present, and give impetus to the creation of an institution, which ... though presently missing, should be set up.

This institution, besides the professional benefit, promises two results: it could be the factor in bringing about the appreciation of Judaism in those in our country who are ignorant of our past and our aspiration, and could support the self-respect of our co-religionists. But most of all, it would be the respectable and lasting creation of our Jewish people, of Jewish generosity and intellectual ambition which, with its generally scientific and artistic importance, is deeply imbued in the upgoing walls of our national education."[9]

At this time, then, there is no talk about the Museum being an independent institution. As it is being planned, it is still the creation and arm of the Hungarian Israelite Literary Society. As indicated, they modify the HILS (IMIT) bylaws too, partly by the insertion of the following text: "The collection of objects, pictures and documents bearing on the history of Hungarian Jewry, its intellectual life, its religious cult, and the establishment and maintenance of a museum that serves the purpose" is part, then, of HILS' responsibilities. Expenses connected with the maintenance of the Museum become in part the burden of HILS itself, but they plan a separate Museum Foundation and conclude that the material possessions or collections of the Museum shall be treated as HILS property.

Next, the newly created Commission of the Museum published a call to the community:

"From the Commission of the Hungarian Jewish
Museum in Budapest: Notice to Hungary's
Citizens of the Jewish Faith

The Hungarian Israelite Literary Society has decided to create a Hungarian Jewish Museum in Budapest.

With this decision, the Society wishes to erect in Hungary yet another memorial to its cultural efforts with an enduring and most valuable institution.

The Jewish congregation has always made its creations available to the service of national purposes and has always fulfilled its obligation to the nation in its enthusiastic support of the sciences and arts. The Hungarian Jewish Museum is to be an institution which, above and beyond its *denominational references, with its general scientific worth, will also represent the enrichment of national culture.*

The Jewish Museum is summoned to make the spirit of Jewry's past common treasure. The progressive intellectual activities of Judaism can best be explained by its ancient cultural life which can eloquently testify to the productivity and labor of our often accused denomination and its labor is most worthy of respect also from a national point of view.

The purpose of the Museum will be to collect those objects that are in any way connected with historical Judaism.

For the time being, the Museum shall function within the framework of the Hungarian Israelite Literary Society; it shall exist and function in accordance with its by-laws, but a separate annual fund is needed for its maintenance. Everybody who supports the Museum with gifts, foundations or annual dues that are to be set, can be a member of the *Museum*. In order to organize the Museum, the Hungarian Israelite Literary Society has appointed a *Museum Commission* from its midst.

This Commission accepts the task developing upon it with enthusiasm and trusts that its reliance on the generosity of the Jews of our country is not in vain. The Commission calls on every member of the Hungarian Jewish community to *enable the creation of the Museum, to join the membership of the Museum with annual dues, to enrich its basis with gifts and endowments. And, if anyone possesses an antique object, heirloom, relic linked to Jewish past that has any bearing on Jewish history, science or art, he should donate or lend it to the Hungarian Jewish Museum. The Commission will accept with grateful thanks the most insignificant gift and object* and urges everyone to obtain from his circle the largest number of specimens to start the Museum. The Commission stresses especially that the objects on loan from their owner *will be marked and preserved* as the property of the depositors and their legal successors.

When we are about to embark on the creation of an institution that is greater in significance and cultural interest than anything before, our work is inspired by the hope that our country's Jewry, as so often in the past, will have understanding for it and will support our endeavor generously. It is up to Hungarian Jews to enhance the prestige of the Museum with as many creations as possible from their nation's spiritual movements and prove their denominational self-respect, their devotion to their tradition and spirit with an institution of lasting benefit.

We recommend the cause of the Hungarian Jewish Museum to the loving care of all members of our denomination.

Budapest, in the month of May, 1910.

THE COMMISSION OF THE
HUNGARIAN JEWISH MUSEUM" [10]

The rest of the Notice describes ways of transmitting offers with the instruction that letters and consignments should be sent to the secretary of the Commission Dr. Sándor Mezey, lawyer, Budapest V, Sas utca 6.

As a result of the Notice, a few members of the Commission sent considerable amounts of money as founding members, while others enrolled as supporting members with smaller amounts. Congregations also became regular members. Though not in large numbers, some one-time donations and more or less valuable objects also arrived. However, the most precious collection is that of the Hevrah Kaddishah of Pest that was, temporarily, to be regarded as a loan only. This organization wished to place all its ritual objects in the Museum.[11] To this day, these ritual objects are among the Museum's most valuable exhibits. Collection of objects continued in the ensuing years. For instance, one can read the following in the report of the Hungarian Jewish Museum for the year 1911:

"The experience of the past year shows that the idea of our Museum has struck deep roots in the minds of our denomination. This proves all the more that our effort is sound and viable for, after all, we have not been able to popularize it sufficiently because of our lack of proper tools. The results encourage our Commission to continue to labor—they seem to have assurance of further rich and joyful results."[12] They address a Notice to the Jewish teachers in February of 1913:

"NOTICE
Honored Colleague

Soon a new institution will be added to the cultural creations of Hungarian Jewry which will be called upon to collect objects characteristic of the folklore and culture of Judaism's past and to have them on permanent exhibit in a manner that creates respect in, and instruction for, all.

This institution, already in a state of advance, will be the Hungarian Jewish Museum.

To find those objects and to search them out for the Museum, the Plenary Commission deems the teachers to be the most qualified *to lend their co-operation who, along with the rabbis, are the most attentive observers and best informed of Hungarian Jewish life, past and present.*

As a member of this Preparatory Commission and at its request, I hereby turn to you with fraternal confidence, my respected colleagues, and ask your aid in assembling material. If you please, notify Dr. Ferenc Mezey, Royal Council (Budapest VI, Laudon utca 3), when you know of an individual, family or organization

Matthias Corvinus and Beatrice enter into Buda in 1476. The Jews welcome the King with the Torah scroll and the double tablets of the Ten Commandments. The Jewish delegation is led by Praefectus Jacobus Mendel.
After the lithograph by Béla Vízkelety. 30 × 40 cm. Inventory No.: 64.1775

in possession of objects qualified for the Museum and which could be obtained as gifts or could be purchased for permanent showing or else, would you inform the undersigned in writing describing accurately and in detail those objects so that, with you, honored colleagues, we can undertake the necessary steps.

We enclose a list of objects that would qualify for inclusion in the Jewish Museum by which our honored colleagues can be guided.

With patriotic, co-religionist and fraternal greetings,

Bernát Mandl,
Budapest VII, Wesselényi utca 44".[13]

It follows logically from the above text that the country's rabbis also received a similar Notice. However, this has not been preserved in the Museum's archives. But perhaps even more important than the Notice is that Mandl discloses the type of material that is needed for the Museum.

"*Ceremonial objects of the synagogue:* Antique, or artistically executed: drapery, table covers [*Mapah*], Torah rollers [*Atze Hayyim*], Torah mantles, Torah binders, silver Torah ornaments: crowns, breastplates, finials with little bells [*Rimmonim*], pointers (metal, bone, wood), Megillah cases, Shofar, Kiddush cups, spice boxes [*Besammim* boxes], Havdallah candle holders, Menorahs, lavers for Levites and pitchers, Huppah, bridal kerchiefs, Elijah's seat and footstool, circumcision knife [Mohel knife], *Halitza* slipper [used when a Levirite marriage is Halakhically avoided], etc.

Ceremonial objects of the family: Sabbath lamp, Kiddush cup, Hallah cover [bread cover], Shalah Manot tray [gifts tray of Purim], Mezuzah holder, etc.

Objects of folklore with inscription or engraving: seals, rings, charms, tops, Hevrah [burial society] pitchers, collection cups or trays, Haman rattles, walking sticks with Hebrew inscription, coins, Pidyan medals [used for redeeming the first-born], other medals with Jewish reference.

Graphic art: Torah scrolls, Megillah scrolls, Haggadah, Shiviti [text facing the minister] and Mizrah [East] plaques, old engagement and marriage contracts, documents, family trees, *El Male Rahamim* [God full of mercy] for martyrs, regulations [*Judenordnung*] of a Jewish community set up by the landlord, official documents filled out for Jewish soldiers, etc.

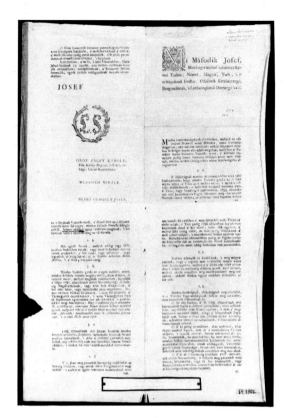

Printed matter : Hebrew or Jewish matter printed by the University of Buda or other Hungarian press, Jewish school books and equipment of national Jewish schools in the Joseph II era. Documents and printed matter relative to the Tolerance Tax, Jewish tax receipts, old wedding invitations [*Chassenebrief*].

Pictures : of synagogues, schools, rabbis, noted personalities of Jewish history, of Jewish family life, of Jewish soldiers, of Jewish costumes."

By 1913 the Museum was ready to look for premises in which to show its collection to the general public. At first, the place found was very modest—three rooms of a rented apartment. But the collection was already significant. The year's most important, new acquisition was a document of the House of Árpád. (This, unfortunately, was lost during World War II, and only a photographic copy survives.) The Museum also acquired a few very important documents dealing with Jewish participation in the 1848–49 War of Independence.

The rooms were slowly furnished. It is characteristic of the Museum staff's professional ambitions that before the Museum was officially open, they had already prepared a descriptive catalog (1915). Miksa Weisz described the books, manuscripts, and the Holy Ark drapes; Bertalan Kolbach the silver, bronze, iron, wood and bone objects; Bernát Mandl the medals and coins, while Bertalan Fabó treated the etchings and pictures. The catalog appeared in two parts in the Hungarian Israelite Literary Society Yearbooks and an offprint was also prepared.[14]

Joseph II's Jewish edict to acquire surnames.
Printed matter. Inventory No.: 64.1906

The official opening took place in the presence of the HILS (IMIT) presidium, members of the Museum Commission, the organizers and Bertalan Fabó, Curator of the Museum, on January 23, 1916. The inauguration address was delivered by Ferenc Mezey, Vice-President of the National Bureau, who pointed out that in a time of destruction, building has heightened significance. He also said that though the Museum was still a new and modest institution, its collection of 1,500 pieces was already worthy of attention. He did not hope that fast development could be expected because of the war, but "as a place that makes up for a specific gap in our country's collections, the Museum will become the small but prized home of the nation's historical and artistic culture".[15]

During the opening year the collection was enlarged by additional 150 objects. The Jewish press was very helpful. For decades before the opening, Miksa Szabolcsi had been working hard on establishment of the Museum, and József Patai, the editor of the illustrated periodical *Múlt és Jövő* (Past and Future), worked diligently on promoting attendance at the Museum by regularly featuring illustrations of its exhibits. Though the measure of the Museum's growth and worth was affected by the ongoing war, its material nevertheless increased gradually and smoothly. The Yearbooks of HILS (IMIT) reported regularly on items purchased by the Museum or received as gifts.

Bertalan Fabó, Curator of the Museum, died in 1921. Fabó's response to everything of cultural value, his unmatched diligence and his expertise were a grave loss. At the annual meeting of the Museum Commission, it was moved to have a Directorate head the Museum in the persons of Miksa Weisz, Bernát Mandl and Bertalan Kohlbach. However, Mandl did not accept his nomination on the grounds that since the lion's share of the work had been done by Miksa Weisz, he should be the one to receive the title of Director. The physician Frigyes Kürschner, who handled the collection selflessly through the years, was elected Curator.[16]

Even during the twenties, a time of slow development, the Museum was not rid of its difficulties. Financial problems were constant. At times the Museum could not even pay its rent. (The apartment in Hold utca presented other difficulties as well. The landlord did not approve of the Museum and when the collection was enlarged with a few headstones, which were placed in the courtyard, he dispatched an attorney's order to have the stones removed immediately on the grounds that the Museum rented the apartment only and not the courtyard. He also threatened legal action.)[17]

We know little of the Museum's activities during this period. The HILS Yearbooks, which had regularly reported the Museum's work, did not appear for years. Documents dated from this time are almost completely missing from the Museum's archives and our data and knowledge is therefore minimal. We must therefore conclude that no significant progress or change took place. When the HILS Yearbook reappeared in 1929, Miksa Weisz's report made fleeting mention of the harsh circumstances, adding that thanks to Ferenc Székely, the Museum Commission's first Chairman, the collection had not become homeless.[18] We also learn from the report that with the assistance of Miksa Weisz, Bernát Mandl, Bertalan Kohlbach and Frigyes Kürschner, the Museum's learned associates had begun to set up a catalog card system. Alas, not much is left of this work!

Still, there was a decisive occurrence in the Museum's life in 1921. The Museum Commission held a session, where Lajos Szabolcsi[19] spoke up and related that, as far as he knew, the Israelite Congregation of Pest (ICP) had building plans. They had decided to build a small synagogue and a cultural center on the vacant lot next to the temple in Dohány utca. Accordingly, room should be requested for the Museum in the cultural center, he said, and he advised immediate negotiations.[20]

No significant change took place till the need arised in 1929 or 1930 (the sources mention these two dates) to vacate the apartment in Hold utca. The collection was crated and placed in the secondary school in Wesselényi utca.[21]

With this, the Museum ceased temporarily. Its material inexpertly crated, it was threatened with ruin. But those who knew the importance of the Museum's existence and its purpose did not give up the fight and negotiated its rejuvenation.

But from the time of Lajos Szabolcsi's statement that next to the Dohány Temple a cultural center was to be built by the Israelite Congregation of Pest, a great many years had to elapse till building was actually commenced. However, it was worth the wait, for finally a three-story building with spacious rooms, suitable for exhibitions, was erected on the basis of plans by László Vágó and Ferenc Faragó.[22] Its execution followed faithfully the synagogue's Moorish style: the façade's ornamentation alternates dark and light bricks, the window decoration is identical with that of the synagogue windows, and the domes placed on top are small copies of the main one. The whole is made one with the Temple. Thus, looking at it from Dohány utca, one cannot differentiate between the synagogue, which was consecrated in 1859 (and whose architect was Ludwig Förster), and the new cultural center, which was finished in 1931.

In the meanwhile, the Museum Commission succeeded in coming to an agreement with the leadership of the ICP at the cost of many difficulties. According to this agreement, the Museum could establish itself on the second floor while the congregational library was to be situated on the third floor. Furthermore, an understanding was arrived at with the Hungarian Israelite Literary Society[23] by which all the material that had been till now regarded as in its trust passed into the possession of a new association when in 1931 the Museum Commission was dissolved and the National Hungarian Jewish Museum Science and Arts Association was formed. The Association was autonomic. The by-laws were approved by the Minister of the Interior on September 19, 1931 under Paragraph No. 134,869 (VII) 1931. The ICP and HILS jointly maintained the Museum financially and both deputed members to the new Association.[24] Adolf Wertheimer[25] became President of the new Association, and Ernő Munkácsi its Secretary.[26] When the cultural center was finished except for a final paint job, the collection was transferred from the school in Wesselényi utca. The silver objects were cleaned, their damage repaired, and paintings restored. Care was given to the seals and plaques, and the Ketubot (marriage contracts) were also repaired. Woven material was restored, the majority of it stretched on frames for exhibition.

It was decided to place all the objects and documents connected with Hungarian Jewish history in the first gallery, the second was to house private and other antiques, and the third was to be the home of ceremonial objects. Despite the agreement that the Museum was entitled to space on the second floor only, the pictures and paintings were put in the first room of the third floor.

Furnishings and restoration cost too much money. It was therefore decided to decorate the Museum windows with stained glass displaying the donors' names. Of these the ornate windows of the east wall in the second gallery—the largest of all the rooms—were completed (and, miraculously, they went unscathed during the siege of Budapest).[27]

The rejuvenated Jewish Museum was opened on December 26, 1932, in the course of a gala general meeting. After Adolf Wertheimer's opening speech,[28] Ödön Gerő delivered a talk in memory of Izsák Perlmutter.[29] The blessing was given by Chief Rabbi Simon Hevesi.[30] Participants in the gala general meeting heard various reports. This was probably the time when Ernő Naményi first became engaged in working for the Museum. His interest in, responsiveness to, and knowledge of, Jewish art stimulated the activities in years to come.

Ernő Munkácsi had already said at the 1931 general meeting that the leadership of the Museum had decided to start exhibiting the moment the building was finished, irrespective of the collection's slow growth through the years.[31] The hope was that the collection, though not complete, would inspire people to donate further objects to the Museum for exhibition purposes.

They were not disappointed. The most important gift was painter Izsák Perlmutter's bequest. According to the artist's will, very valuable paintings and real estate became Museum property (e.g., the Andrássy út 60 block of flats which later was the headquarters of the Arrow Cross party, and the Perlmutter mansion in Rákospalota, which was immortalized in a beautiful painting). On the other hand, the list of purchased items is very short. Listing of the donated objects, however, is almost eleven printed pages long in the 1933 HILS Yearbook.[32] Many among them are valuable gifts as, for instance, the donation of the above-mentioned Biblical theme lead-glass windows which decorate the galleries to this day. However, the museum was always short of money; regular purchases and planned growth were always in small measure, and the private donations of objects often of little or no value.

This is how it was from the beginning and—regrettably—this is how it is today. Yet the leaders of the Museum felt at the beginning of the 1930s that the main mission of the Museum was to awaken and to maintain Jewish historical self-respect because that is tied up with Jewish life-ambition and is more important than "the collection of treasures with absolute artistic values".[33] Awakening and strengthening of Jewish self-respect was indeed the mission of every Jewish institution during those days of increasing blows to the Jews.

In 1932, in connection with opening the building, the leaders of the Museum enumerated once again the purposes of their work of gathering material.[34] Furthermore, they decided to start collecting relics of synagogue art and privately owned antiques. For the former, they intended to turn to congregations and Havurot (fraternities) and for the latter, to use the denominational press in popularizing the idea. They wished to collect memorabilia of outstanding Hungarian Jews.

A few months later, in the summer of 1933, the Museum Association held a general meeting in which Ernő Munkácsi recalled the situation of Germany's Jews, in moving words and, in reference to that, spoke of the danger with which the German Jewish individual, Jewish science and art were faced.

The situation lent added importance to the role of Hungarian Jewry and within it, the Museum, cautioned Munkácsi, who once again stressed the importance of the historical collection in these words: "Our Museum exercises its most profound influence with its historical collection. The Jewish visitor leaves with a heightened sense of self-respect for he has seen in the Museum's first gallery the documents bearing witness to our thousand-year-old Hungarian Jewish history, starting with relics of the Árpád era, while the non-Jew receives instruction and thus feels respect for Judaism, because under the weight of proof accusations leveled at the recent immigration of Jews and its detrimental effects on the Hungarians' collapse. We can say, indeed, saxa loquuntur—our Museum's historical collection is convincing. We can learn from it that Hungarian Jewry has always been a beneficial and historically joined part of the Hungarian State and Hungarian society."[35]

We can report great development after 1932, when growth fostered by the decision of the Israelite Congregation of Pest (ICP) to move its library, originally situated on the third floor of the building, making room for the so-called Historical Portrait Gallery exhibiting oil paintings, statues and photographs of noteworthy Jewish Hungarians, as well as an art exhibition. Doubtless, this growth was the result of sad changes. The world at large became more and more antagonistic toward the Jew; first it isolated, later excluded the individual from all areas of social, economic and cultural life. This caused the natural reaction of turning inward. There was no stage for Jewish dramatists and actors. Therefore, there was a need for the foundation of a Jewish theater. There was no possibility for Jewish artists to exhibit their art, and so no hope of selling it, so conditions had to be created. Magazines did not publish writings of Jewish authors, so Jewish periodicals had to be started. Since scientific and popular lectures were most often anti-Semitic, lecture series had to be organized. If the world at large was turning into a sad place, there had to be a forum where this could be remedied.

That is the reason for the formation of OMIKE (Országos Magyar Izraelita Közművelődési Egyesület —National Hungarian Israelite Cultural Association).[36] It had its separate theater and staged shows by excellent authors. The operatic presentations of the theater were packed, so were cabaret entertainments which provided some comfort in a joyless life. The Museum's exhibitions grew in number and masses of books with Jewish content—some of them of excellent quality—and the outstanding monthly Libanon were published.

Let us now consider the Museum's temporary exhibitions. At the beginning, there was no possibility of organizing special showings—there was no room in the confined quarters of the Hold utca flat. But in 1937, when the exhibition of the historical portrait gallery and the Perlmutter bequest were opened on a permanent basis, a collection of photographs consisting of several hundred items on the synagogue treasures of Italian Jewish communities was put on temporary display. But the first really significant seasonal arrangement was the "Emancipation Exhibit" in March, 1938.[37] There is need to stress the obvious relation between the date and the subject of the exhibit. Though the historic situation was fraught with danger, the organizers of the exhibition were still optimistic. They thought they could prove logically and with documents that Jews had lived here for centuries and are an integral part of the country, that is why they selected and showed those documents that indicated the true measure of Jewish participation in the country.

The first important document is the "Golden Bull", the copy of King Béla IV's charter of privilege regulating the Hungarian Jews' legal relations (1251). Endorsement of this from the year 1484 is also on

Lajos Kossuth and Bertalan Szemere's emancipation proclamation, July 28, 1849. Because the War of Independence was suppressed, it was never enforced. Inventory No.: 64.1802

display. The validity of this document was confirmed also by Ladislaus V and Matthias Corvinus. Shown are the lithograph of the entry into Buda by Matthias and Beatrice (1476) and the portrait of Jakab Mendel, the first Jewish prefect, painted by Lipót Gedő after the likeness in the prefect's seal.

The ordinances of Joseph II and Jewish-related applications and ordinances of the end of the 18th and beginning of the 19th centuries are also on display. Special emphasis is given to the first emancipation law entitled "Law Concerning Jews" passed on July 28, 1849[38] in Szeged, and the leaflet praising it.

Important role is given at the exhibition to the Jewish petitions addressed to the Diet from 1790 to 1861 and that part of the 1861 Diet journal in which Kálmán Tisza proposed "enforcement of civil and political equality between denominations, including the Israelites", followed by the Law of Emancipation itself.

The first Jewish books appearing in Hungarian, the first Jewish Bible translation (Móric Bloch, 1840), the first prayerbook in Hungarian translation Jiszráel könyörgései (Supplications of Israel, Móric Rosenthal and Móric Bloch, 1841), the first Hungarian Jewish periodical Magyar Zsinagóga (Hungarian Synagogue, 1847), as well as a few statues and pictures are also displayed in cases. The selection of certificates, documents and other objects was done skilfully to show how the Jewish people's legal standing had been positively influenced, while all those writings that were discriminatory were omitted.

The next exhibition in December, 1939, was not devoid of political references either, despite the fact that it was devoted to art. Galleries were no longer available for Jewish painters and sculptors in 1939; as a consequence, the National Hungarian Israelite Cultural Association Council organized the exhibition, where the era's great Jewish masters came to be shown. In the exhibition catalog we can read illustrious

The Law of Emancipation. 1867. Signatories : Francis Joseph, King of Hungary, and Prime Minister Gyula Andrássy. Printed matter. Inventory No.: 64.1807

names like Endre Bálint, Margit Anna, Imre Ámos, Endre Vadász, István Zádor, Csaba Vilmos Perlrott, Lipót Herman, Armand Schönberger, Ferenc Bolmányi, Rudolf Diener-Dénes, Lajos Vajda, Béla Kádár, Frigyes Frank, painters; István Örkényi Strasser, György Goldmann, Dezső Bokros Birman, István Csillag, sculptors. The creations on display were for sale.[39]

The occasion for the Lipót Lőw Memorial Exhibition came around in September, 1942. This exhibition provided the opportunity for the Museum leadership to show Jewish life and art of a century ago.[40]

At the opening, Fülöp Grünvald delivered his lecture on Lipót Lőw which showed how the originally Moravian Lőw became a Hungarian rabbi, a military chaplain of the War of Liberation, the fighter for Jewish emancipation in the land, a scholar thrown in prison for his defence of Hungarian liberty. At the same time, Ernő Naményi looked back to the people who "laid the foundation of Hungarian Jewry's cultural and economic development and, almost as bereft of rights as we are, were the enthusiastic and hopeful toilers of that age...," so that "we be enabled to bear the bitterness and trials of our time".

The exhibition introduced Lipót Lőw's career and the lives of some of his contemporaries who worked tirelessly for the country's benefit, for Hungarian culture and for the creation of Hungarian industry. In 1943, on the 100th anniversary of the birth of József Kiss, the Museum organized the poet's memorial exhibition.[41] On exhibit were his manuscripts, photographs, letters, and other memorabilia. The visitors were also treated to the illustrations of his poems by such eminent painters as Károly Ferenczy, Béla Iványi Grünwald and Miklós Vadász. An interesting series of photographs showed the circle of writers and poets who had become famous and had been discovered by editor József Kiss, and whose first works had appeared in the columns of the periodical Hét (Week).

Also in 1943, the Museum provided a home for the creative arts group of the National Hungarian Israelite

XX. CZIKK.

Hitel- és biztosító intézetek engedélyezése azon ministeriumot illeti, melynek államterületén az illető társulat székhelyét választja; ha azonban működését a másik államterületre is ki akarja terjeszteni, alapszabályainak előmutatása mellett az ez iránti engedélyt az ottani ministeriumnál köteles megszerezni.

XXI. CZIKK.

A második czikkben érintett nemzetközi kereskedelmi szerződések, a vámok, a közvetett adók, és az ezen vám- és kereskedelmi szövetségben foglalt egyéb tárgyak egyforma alapjainak előkészitése és közvetitése végett, vám- és kereskedelmi értekezlet fog egybegyülni, melyet a két részről való kereskedelmi és pénzügyi ministerek, s a mennyiben a tanácskozás tárgya a külfölddel való viszonyt érinti, a közös külügyminister, illetőleg mindezek helyetesei képeznek, s a melyhez, a hányszor a tárgy megkivánja, mindkét államterületbeli szakférfiak a különösen kereskedelmi kamarai tagok hivatnak meg.

Mindkét fél ministeriumai fel vannak jogositva, valahányszor szükségesnek tartják, a vám- és kereskedelmi értekezlet egybehivását igénybe venni.

XXII. CZIKK.

E vám- és kereskedelmi szövetség a kihirdetés napján s 10 évi időre lép érvénybe, s ha fel nem mondatik, további 10 évre, s igy 10 évről 10 évre folyton fennállónak ismertetik el. A felmondás mindenkor csak a 9-ik év végén történhetik meg, s ez esetben a szerződés megujitása iránti egyezkedés hasonló uton haladék nélkül megkezdendő.

Mindazonáltal a szerződési idő öt első évének elteltével mindenik félnek szabadságában álland e határozványok megváltoztatására alkudozást inditványozni, mely alkudozást a másik fél vissza nem utasithat. Ha ez uton az egyessége 6 hónap alatt el nem érhető, mindkét fél szabadságában áll egy évi felmondással elni. Ez esetben a szerződés megujitása iránti egyezkedés haladék nélkül megkezdendő.

Ha e szerződés egyes határozmányi azonnal nem lennének végrehajthatók, a két részről való felelős ministeriumok a szükséges átmeneti intézkedéseket közös egyetértéssel fogják megállapitani.

XVII.

Törvényczikk

az izraeliták egyenjogúságáról polgári s politikai jogok tekintetében.

1. §.

Az ország izraelita lakosai a keresztény lakosokkal minden polgári és politikai jog gyakorlására egyaránt jogositottaknak nyilvánittatnak.

2. §.

Minden ezzel ellenkező törvény, szokás, vagy rendelet ezennel megszüntettetik.

XVIII.

Törvényczikk

az 1868. év első évharmada folytán viselendő közterhekről.

1. §.

Addig is, mig az 1867. 12. t. cz. 40. szakasza értelmében a közös költségek fedezésére szükséges összegek meghatározása után az államköltségvetés a jövő évre előterjesztetik, és törvényhozási tárgyalás folytán megállapittatik: a magyar korona országaiban jelenleg fennálló összes, egyenes és közvetett adók, ugy szintén az államegyedárusságok, a jövő 1868. évi január 1-től kezdve, ugyanazon évi april hó 30-káig a folyó 1867. évre országos határozat által ideiglenesen elfogadott rendszer szerint, érvényben maradnak.

2. §.

Ha ez időközben bármely adónemre nézve törvényhozási intézkedés jő létre: az, a törvénynek a hivatalos lapban (Budapesti Közlöny) történt közzétetele után, a törvényben magában kijelölt napon és mód szerint életbe lép.

3. §.

Az 1-ső szakaszban megállapitott 4 havi időszak alatt a pénzügyminister a beligazgatási költségek fedezésére a jelen év folytán gyakorlatban volt eljárás szerint fogja a szükséges összegeket folyókká tenni.

12

Cultural Association (OMIKE). Admittedly, one of the purposes of the exhibition was to ease the artists' poverty. Because of that—and it can be presumed, only because of that—was it possible to have inferior work shown along with masterpieces.[42]

"The purpose," writes Ernő Naményi, the director of the Museum, in his report on the exhibition, "is to show how Jewish artists have enriched the Hungarian fine arts, has been accomplished only partially, first and foremost because one cannot classify creative artists only by their religious affiliation." Naményi's opinion is altogether correct. Permanent showing of creative art in the Museum ceased because of that principle (and if the reader comes across paintings in this volume, it is because they are in the Museum's possession, but the majority is not exhibited). Plaques of prominent Jewish personalities are also included in the Museum's collection.

Mention should be made of the periodical titled *Libanon*. In the beginning, *Libanon* was not yet a publication of the Museum. It appears as the Jewish scientific and critical monthly, the *Zsidó Tudományos és Kritikai Folyóirat* under the editorship of József M. Grózinger, Zoltán Kohn and Jenő Zsoldos. Afterwards, however, it was transformed into the Museum organ and, from then on, was published with the subtitle, "National Hungarian Jewish Museum Science and Art Association's Science and Art Monthly". Its editor-in-chief (Ernő Munkácsi) and editorial board selected their articles in good taste and with a critical eye, including some important studies and shorter, but just as important, book reviews. From the time when the dignified periodical became the official organ of the Museum, many photographs of Museum objects appeared, as well as texts of documents owned by the Museum, and articles describing the Museum's holdings. In order to have an idea of the way the magazine publicized the Museum, we wish to quote two numbers, chosen at random.

Volume VII (1942), No. 1:

In this number is found Ernő Naményi's important study on Herend Seder plates, among them also those owned by the Museum. The periodical also published the photographs of a few plates. At the time of publication of the article, the Museum had only two Herend plates. There appear, however, photographs of two other Seder plates that afterwards also became part of the collection. This number also includes the study by György Balázs, the very talented member of the Museum who died in World War II, on the wooden synagogue of Náznánfalva. This included the text of documents relating to the synagogue. The wooden synagogue's remaining few pieces are still on exhibit at the Museum.

Volume VI (1942), No. 3:

The first article is Sándor Büchler's report on a codex fragment kept in the Festetics Library in Keszthely illustrating Eve, the Serpent, and partially Adam. The drawing was executed in micro-graphic technique using the letters of a Hebrew text. Büchler is of the opinion (according to Alexander Scheiber, in error) that it dates back no later than the 14th century. It is possible that the leaders of the Museum knew even at the time of publication of the article that the codex fragment would eventually become Museum property. The periodical also printed photographs of the parchment fragment and the

Ede Telcs : Lipót Lőw. Terracotta.
Inventory No.: 64.2641

terracotta statue of Lipót Lőw by Ede Telcs. This is the number in which the mentioned biographical sketch of Fülöp Grünvald is featured. Important documents linked with Hungarian Jewish past and kept at the Museum appear in Fülöp Grünvald's and Jenő Zsoldos's article. Present is also a report on the general meeting and that of the directors for the year 1941–1942.

Speaking of publications, we should also mention the documentary brochure *Ítéljetek* (You Judge), edited by Márton Vida. The aim of the brochure is to show—in popular style—with photographs how much the country's Jews considered themselves Hungarian and how much they had done for Hungarian economic and cultural development. *Ítéljetek*—which could not accomplish its purpose to counteract anti-Semitic tendencies—was not a publication of the Museum, but its material was almost entirely taken from it. In 1939, to be able to vote, Jews had to prove that their ancestors had lived in Hungary for the last one hundred years. To prove this, there was a rush of "ancestor search". The Museum had in its possession the photo-copies of Hungary's conscriptions (census). Many Jews turned to the Museum in an effort to find ancestors in the census of the 18th and 19th centuries.

At the end of the 1930s and the beginning of the 1940s, many Hungarian Jewish organizations presented lectures of Jewish content. The so-called Free University advertised a series of three lectures in the Museum to present its material.[43]

The first lecturer was Ernő Naményi. His talk was on the subject of the development of Jewish religious art. He stated that the Museum did not possess any religious art older than the 16th century because objects of prior age had been destroyed in the course of various wars. Auditors of the lecture viewed the ceremonial objects with great interest and listened to the accompanying explanations. On the second occasion, Fülöp Grünvald spoke about Hungarian Jewish historical memorabilia. He introduced the Museum's historical material : documents from the Middle Ages, old gravestones, Hungarian coins of the House of Árpád era with Hebrew letters on them, patents of protection by landlords and, finally, those documents that illustrate the process of change into citizenship and the struggle for equal rights and self-regulation. In the course of the third lecture, György Balázs spoke of antiquities and the results of excavations—the Jewish headstone of the third century found in Esztergom, the votive plaque that came from Dunaújváros also of the third century, the gravestone of Albertirsa and the Roman lamp decorated with a Menorah.

The Museum's enthusiastic leaders even had the time and energy to circulate a few works of art. They issued the medal of Prefect Mendel by István Örkényi Strasser who later died a martyr's death, the copper plate portrait of Mózes Münz, Chief Rabbi of Óbuda, etched by Lenhard who copied Donáth's painting that had the old plate as its original and, last, a white silk print cake cover of which the design and Hebrew letters were done by Albert Kner.

The permanent exhibition was well attended. There were well prepared important seasonal exhibitions, a periodical, participation in the edition of various publications, circulating of objects of art, and lecture series. It was an era of activity without equal in the history of the Museum. It came to an end in 1942 with the Museum's leaders judiciously deciding to draw up plans for hiding the collection. The most valuable and jealously guarded objects were once more crated. Dr. Magda Bárány Oberschall and Gabriella Tápai Szabó, colleagues in the Hungarian National Museum, hid the sealed crates full of art treasures in the cellar of the National Museum. They put the old irreplaceable documents in bank-vaults.

And so, another era came to an end. The real treasures were now missing from the galleries. After the German occupation, there was an attempt made to take an inventory of the remaining objects, but part of the material was taken away by the notorious Jewish Research Institute. Later, the building became the center of forced labor batallions. Even then the Museum had a mission: it provided roof over the heads of forced laborers. This had special importance because some workers tried to take advantage of the very limited possibilities of providing assistance—they carried news and letters back and forth between the inhabitants of the ghetto that was just taking shape. They smuggled parcels into the ghetto and extended help to Jews arrested in the streets and dragged there. And when the members of the Arrow Cross packed the Jews into the Dohány Street Temple prior to deportation, so that the forced march to Austria and the German empire could start from there, the wall shared by the Temple and the Museum was secretly broken through. The Temple was closed from the direction of Dohány Street by the Arrow Cross and the Jews were driven from Síp utca through the back wing into the Temple building. However, those who tried to escape to the women's gallery found the breached wall and reached the Museum whose door fell outside the territory of the closed ghetto. People who thus reached the "free" street escaped—at least for the time being.

The Museum that had delighted, instructed and strengthened Jewish self-respect through the years now saved lives during the most tragic period of Hungarian Jewry, the winter of 1944.

It stands to reason that the rebuilding of the Museum could not be started immediately after the liberation of the country. To assist individuals, to tidy up synagogues, to start work in hospitals again, to create homes for children left without parents, were more urgent missions. Consequently, repairs on the Museum building were begun only in 1947. Expenses were covered by the American Joint Distribution Committee[44] and the Israelite Congregation of Pest.[45] Repairs proceeded well, and by early summer of the same year, the crates holding the collection's most precious treasures—hidden in the National Museum's cellar during the war—were already within the walls of the Museum. According to one report, the arrival of the crates was accompanied by anxious moments.[46] The Museum's directors, Ernő

The speech of Lipót Lőv (correct spelling: Lőw), Chief Rabbi in Pápa, addressed to the Jewish soldiers of the War of Independence while encamped. Booklet. Printed in Pápa by using the characters of the Calvinist Academy. 1848. Inventory No.: 64.1416

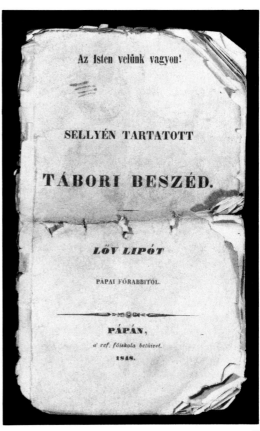

Naményi and Fülöp Grünvald, ascertained that the seals were intact and then opened the crates. First, a spice box emerged and then, in good order, the Museum's most valuable objects, none missing. However, the material placed in the bank's safe—which had been broken into—was gone. Important and significant documents, among them early-medieval deeds of the House of Árpád (9th–13th centuries) were lost and have never been found.

The Museum's leaders and their co-workers now prepared for the third opening. This came about on July 4, 1947.[47] The rededication was an impressive festivity attended by such notables as Culture Minister Gyula Ortutay, Information Minister Ernő Mihályfi, Secretary of State for Culture László Bóka, Ministerial Counselors László Kardos and Sándor Simon, University Professor Tibor Gerevich, General Director Lajos Huszár, Private Docent Magda Bárány Oberschall, Director of the National Museum Sándor Mihalik, Director of the Budapest Museum of Fine Arts István Genthon, and Ferenc Szoboszlay Counsel of Education for the Capital City of Budapest. Representing the Jewish community were the presidium of the National Bureau, the European chairman of the AJDC and the leaders of its Hungarian office, as well as leaders of various other institutions and organizations.

The arriving guests were greeted by Ernő Naményi, who in his talk sketched the collection's fate during the war and related that the Jewish Research Institute had robbed part of the collection, and a number of air attacks also contributed to the destruction of the material left in the building. Invaluable pieces disappeared without a trace. The only part of the collection that remained intact was the one that was hidden by a few workers of the National Museum.

In his moving speech, Gyula Ortutay spoke of the destruction that took place and of the guilt every decent person must feel. He would take greater joy in the opening—he said—if the National Museum would have brought not only dead matter but also living people. "I may state in the government's name," he assured all, "that we wish to work towards the end that nobody shall ever suffer on account of race in this land again."

Joe Swartz spoke in the name of the Joint Distribution Committee. Besides charitable work, the Joint's activities—he said—encompassed the cultural sphere, too, and the Committee wished to serve the spirit of Judaism. That is why it had also assisted in rebuilding the Museum.

In 1948, there was another organizational change in the Museum. To maintain and direct it, the Science and Arts Association of the National Hungarian Jewish Museum and Library was brought into being. Its president, the actual director of the Museum, was Ernő Naményi. The constitution of the new association was prepared and approved by the Minister of the Interior on April 3rd.[48]

The new association drafted its purposes again: "The collection of objects related to the Jewish People's history, religious cult, synagogue arrangement, intellectual and economic life, artifacts—specially with Hungarian reference—books, documents, pictures and other objects; maintaining a museum and library for the purpose; the organization of lectures in the capital city and smaller towns on or related to the above objects; the publication of scientific works and works on the history of art; further, the organization of seasonal exhibitions of the objects, and assistance of scientific research related to such objects." A precise and huge plan. What a pity that apart from maintenance of the Museum, nothing came of it. True enough, the association functioned for a short time only. After about two years' activity, it discontinued to operate and the Museum was taken over by the Central Board of Hungarian Jews. However, prior to that, the association did organize a few important exhibitions.

Three exhibitions were advertised in 1949. There was a showing of Hungarian synagogue art on the occasion of the 90th anniversary of the Dohány utca Temple.[49] The collection of photographs of synagogues, started for that exhibition, augmented many times since then, is today one of the major collections of the Museum, all the more so since many synagogues were destroyed during World War II. Furthermore, as a consequence of the war, synagogues of towns and villages depopulated of Jews had been abandoned and left to decay.

The portraits of the Dohány Temple's former rabbis, their manuscripts and literary works were placed in the first gallery. In the second gallery, photographs of the most important relics of synagogue architecture in Hungary were displayed: the most important Hungarian examples of synagogue style developed in Poland —with four pillars in the center, such as the synagogues of Mád, Zsámbék, Apostag, Bonyhád, as well as the so-called Wertheimer Temple of Kismarton from the 18th-century, the early 19th-century temple from Nagykanizsa, and another Kismarton synagogue, both of which illustrate the classicist taste of the times; the temple of Óbuda, the most beautiful classicist synagogue in Hungary; the synagogue of the same era from Hunfalva and the temple in Várpalota, the building of which was influenced by the Óbuda Temple; the first synagogue in Pest; the Orczy-ház synagogue; the Ark (Aron) with its Hungarian coat of arms in the old Szeged synagogue; the first three-nave synagogue built in 1846 in Pápa; the Rumbach utca temple, a witness to the spirit of romanticism; the Gothic style Buda-Újlak synagogue; the synagogues designed by Lipót Baumhorn; the synagogues of Szeged, of Aréna út (now Dózsa György út), Páva utca, Csáky utca (now Hegedűs Gyula utca) and Bethlen tér. Next to the photographs of some country town synagogues, pictures of two modern buildings were also on display: the Heroes' Temple and the Buda Lágymányos Temple. The final items of the exhibit were the photographs of the synagogue in Dohány utca. Other famous synagogues were also represented, for instance, the fresco-decorated Dura-Europos synagogue, the 13th-century five-nave Toledo synagogue, and the 11th-century Worms synagogue which had fallen on "*Kristallnacht*".[50] The exhibition was open for only two weeks; nevertheless, the number of visitors was rather high—about 1,400. The fact is that its popularity was heightened by the showing of Lipót Herman's winged altar inspired by the Biblical Ezekiel, Chapter 37 —the consoling vision of the destroyed but resurrected House of Israel. This was later moved abroad.

The Museum also advertised plans for an antifascist exhibit. However, there was not enough material for that. It continued collecting material, and the exhibition was held much later.

When the leaders of the Hungarian Jewish community decided to end institutional autonomy and make the institutions part of the Israelite Congregation of Budapest made up of the formerly individually functioning congregations (i.e., the orphanages), or merge them with the Central Board of Hungarian Jews (Magyar Izraeliták Országos Irodája), the Museum also changed into an institution of the CBHJ. From

A piece from the wooden synagogue in Náznánfalva. Painted. Inventory No.: 66.8

then on, its name changed too: National Jewish Religious and Historical Collection. But the public continued to refer to it as the Jewish Museum.

Documents related to the building of the Dohány utca Temple, the Temple's beautiful *Parokhot* (Holy Ark curtains), the old, wonderful Ark curtains of Óbuda, very many silversmith articles and also the few remaining pieces of the wooden synagogue of Náznánfalva were also part of the exhibition. The Museum also published a brochure in which appeared József Katona's study on the 90-year-old Dohány utca Temple and that of Fülöp Grünvald and Ernő Naményi on Budapest's other synagogues.[51]

Also in 1949 were prepared a beautiful catalog and invitation to the "Art of the Seder" exhibition, whose principal aim was to show the development of Haggadah art.[52] The oldest example shown was the 10th-century Haggadah fragment found in the Cairo Geniza[53] and now the property of the National Rabbinical Seminary. The oldest printed Haggadah in the exhibit was printed in Constantinople in 1514–1516.

Beside the many old printed Haggadot, modern ones were also present and, of course, those made in Hungary, too. The visitors were treated to the sight of many Seder trays (e.g., the tray made in Pesaro in 1652), rare pewter plates, Seder cups and Seder tray covers.

The opening years were not especially lucky. Ernő Naményi, who had been so active till then and knew so much about art, left the country. Though Fülöp Grünvald, an outstanding scholar of Hungarian Jewish

A Jew with yellow star reading the poster
ordering Jews to list their movable property.
Photograph

history, became the director, he could not overcome the difficulties. As a matter of fact, since its very existence, the institution had always been treated somewhat like an orphan. Now it was doubly so. There was hardly any money for its upkeep, much less for further development. Thus, when water seeped into the building in many places because of the leaky roof, the Museum had to be closed.

Finally, it was the Conference on Jewish Material Claims Against Germany, Department of Culture and Education, that undertook the cost of organizing the anti-fascist exhibition. This made it possible to attach to the Museum an unused adjoining hall of the temple and present there the exhibition of Hungarian Jewry's saddest epoch, its tragic history under Fascism. At the time of the exhibition, the Israelite Congregation of Pest had the entire building repaired.

The anti-fascist exhibition showed Hungarian Jewry's destruction in chronological order through original documents, photographs and photo-copies. Once again, money to be disposed of was scarce, enlarged photographs or big, easily read posters to show printed texts, placards and leaflets could not be made. Nevertheless, the message of the exhibition was—we thought so then and we still think so today—unmistakable and shocking. Many tens of thousands of visitors, from far and wide, whose countries were spared Hitler's occupation, learned how so many Hungarian Jews perished, and many young people learned here for the first time what Fascism had really meant.

Years passed over the Museum without anything significant happening. There were only three people working in the institution, Fülöp Grünvald and his two colleagues.

In 1963, the direction of the Museum fell to the author of this introductory essay. At long last, an exhibition was organized again in 1966 which presented the drawings of the children of the Theresienstadt camp, on loan from the Jewish Museum of Prague. It was impossible to view these children's drawings without being deeply moved. True, the children's drawings are no works of art, but they were made by children snatched from their homes and deported to the special camp in Theresienstadt. This camp was a "show-place", planned by the Nazis with the intention of proving to commissions of the International Red Cross that the widely spread rumors about dreadful camps were unfounded. The children were not killed on the first day of deportation as it happened at Auschwitz, only much later. For a time, they were allowed to learn, to draw, to remember. In their drawings, they immortalized their memories, their towns, their homes, their lost, peaceful lives.

The exhibition enjoyed extraordinary success and was prolonged. For the first time, the Museum was even featured on television, reports over the radio spoke of the occurrence, and there was hardly an important newspaper or periodical which did not write about the exhibition at some length.

Next year, an exhibition was prepared of Izsák Perlmutter's paintings. The core of the exhibition consisted of the Perlmutter bequest handled by the Museum, complemented by the material on loan from the Hungarian National Gallery. However, after a time, such exhibitions could not be continued. The building's third floor, where temporary exhibits were placed, came into such bad repair that visitors could not be admitted there any more.

For decades, only two permanent exhibitions were on display. The first historical gallery presented the main events of Hungarian Jewish life from its beginnings to the end of World War II. The second historical gallery had the already described anti-fascist exhibit.

No doubt, the historical material is the more important one. From before the establishment of the Museum, its leaders and their appointees had already, methodically and regularly, striven to collect those documents from which the history of Hungarian Jewry could be reconstructed. The oldest piece is a third-century Jewish gravestone. This was found in the last century in the town of Esztergom and came into the collection by way of exchange, since neither the archiepiscopal administration nor the leaders of Jewish cultural life ever had any doubt about its rightful place being in the Jewish Museum (three artifacts from Ödön Faragó's excellent collection were placed in the Christian Musem of Esztergom in exchange of the gravestone). The Esztergom find —containing other stones as well, which, however, are not in the Museum (some, copies though, can be seen there)—proves that Jews have lived on this territory long before the Conquest, when part of the country was a Roman province. We have a few original coins from the time of the first Hungarian kings with the Hebrew initials of the Jewish minter. Copies of parts of codices, touching upon Jewish matters, are also on display. The period of the Conquest is documented with gravestones and a few etchings showing the homes of Jews in Buda. Copies of censuses, *conscripti,* throw light on the number of Jews, their occupations and social standing in various times. The Museum also owns many documents on the so-called Tolerance Tax—the special tax on Jews. There are also petitions written by Jews in which they ask for permission to settle, change occupations or establish a family in times when, in any walk of life, a Jew could inhabit a place or work by special license only.

A woman's dress made of a *Tallit* (prayershawl), stolen after deportation. Photograph

In this introduction, we have quoted Sándor Büchler's article in which he speaks of the archives of the Jews of Óbuda and urges the Óbuda congregation to place that singularly precious material at the disposal of the Jewish Museum. This material has, indeed, come to the Museum, and its importance has since grown, because the archives of all the other congregations were destroyed during World War II. In addition, the "Óbuda Documents" are important because, at the time of their origin (end of 18th and beginning of 19th centuries), Hungarian Jews had no union or organizations as yet, and had to turn in all matters to the leaders of the age's two largest congregations, to those of Pozsony and Óbuda, in the hope of influence and help. Büchler was acquainted with these documents and did much research on them. Their complete publication can be expected in the near future.

Significant are documents of Jewish participation in the War of Independence (1848–1849), and so is the material introducing the Hungarian struggle for emancipation.

The most extensive documentary collection is the one relating to Fascism. Many original sources, copies of manuscripts and hundreds of photographs show how almost 600,000 Hungarian Jews perished. This is the best known part of the historical collection. It offers rich source material for many native and foreign scholars, as well as the mass media.

The Museum's manuscript collection is also important and significant. It contains copies of documents in the possession of various state organizations, scientific notes of noted authors, personal documents and correspondence. There is also a collection of press clippings made up of Jewish related studies and articles that appeared in Hungarian newspapers between the two World Wars. The collection of photographs contains pictures of the old and the 19th and 20th-century Hungarian synagogues. Thus, as mentioned before, photographs of the synagogues destroyed or depopulated during the war and put to different use are at least preserved. Also on display are the portraits of important persons.

Through the years, the state of the building further deteriorated. Water seeped down to the second floor, the exhibits were too crowded, they became difficult to view, and there was not enough money for repairs. A few years ago, however, a decisive change took place. The Hungarian cultural administration came to

Galleries of the exhibition

the conclusion that, because of the value of the collections, including the art treasures, something had to be done, even though the Jewish Museum is not a state institution.

We can never be sufficiently grateful for what they have done. The Ministry of Culture contributed a considerable amount to the reconstruction of the building and the restoration of the art treasures. The Central Directorate of Museums undertook the restoration work, provided new furnishings, and the technicians made reality of all that our scenario has visualized above.

At least, the collection is now in suitable surroundings. The row of lamps inside the showcase illuminate the selected ceremonial objects of Jewish religion. Centrally located in the first gallery is the Torah scroll, the book in its ancient form, a handwritten parchment scroll. Around it and next to the walls line up the scroll's ornaments and all the ritual objects of Sabbath observance, Hungarian and used in Hungary. Decorated synagogue curtains, beautifully embroidered textile fabrics heighten the loveliness of the hall.

The next gallery displays the ceremonial objects of the Festivals, selected so that they represent the masterpieces of Hungarian applied and industrial art. The most notable are the Seder plates made in the world-famous Herend china factory. We stress especially the collection of Hanukkah light and candlelamps and a few very beautiful miniature, handwritten, illustrated prayerbooks.

Having become acquainted with the Sabbath and Festival ceremonial objects, the visitor is next introduced to the ritual objects used on weekdays, as well as those the religious Jews use on the occasion of a birth, wedding or death.

Even from among these, the pretty, handwritten, illustrated marriage contracts and a special codex are outstanding. This extensive codex, illustrated on all pages, was made at the end of the 18th century in Nagykanizsa. Both its text and its illustration deserve special attention (its marginal illustrations reflect the influence of Hungarian folk art).

The possibilities of obtaining further financial assistance have been exhausted, however, and so, for the time being, the historical exhibition cannot be organized. Today, only a fraction of that material can be seen (as, for example, the 3rd-century gravestone).

The exhibition showing the Hungarian Jewish tragedy during World War II presents documents, photographs, newspaper articles. A photograph or two illustrate the period of the Jewish laws, forced labor, deportation, the concentration camps, the Budapest ghetto and its liberation, and the final calling to account of war criminals. The exhibition ends with the Provisional Government's decree, appearing immediately after the liberation, voiding all fascist anti-Semitic ordinances, and closes with the paragraph of the Constitution designating anti-Semitism as a punishable act. The provisional exhibition's many photographs mirror Jewish life in Budapest today.

The quality of the collection, the beauty of its harmonious setting, the unity of its presentation, all make the Jewish Museum of Budapest one of the most beautiful Jewish museums in Europe.

This volume introduces the collection's most important and most outstanding pieces.

NOTES

1. Bernát Alexander: *A Millenniumi Kiállításon* [At the Millennial Exhibition]. *Izraelita Magyar Irodalmi Társulat Évkönyve* [The Hungarian Israelite Literary Society Yearbook, henceforth referred to by its Hungarian acronym "IMIT"], Budapest, 1897, 43–48.
2. Izsák Schulhof: *Budai Krónika* [Chronicle of Buda]. From the Hebrew by László Jólesz, Budapest, 1979.
3. Miksa Szabolcsi: "Zsidó Gyűjtemények Tára" [The Corpus of Jewish Collections], *Egyenlőség* XV [1896], No. 33, 4-6.
4. Ibid.
5. Sándor Büchler: "Az alapítandó zsidó múzeum dolgában" [In the Matter of the Jewish Museum to be Established], *Egyenlőség* XV [1896], No. 40, 2–4.
Sándor Büchler, Chief Rabbi in Keszthely, University Private Docent, Researcher of Hungarian Jewish History.
6. The Hungarian Israelite Literary Society (IMIT) was founded in 1894. Its purpose was the publication of Jewish religious and learned literature, the organization of public lectures, setting up of competitions and the awarding of prizes. It publishes the annual yearbook which popularizes learned studies, short stories and poems. The first Hungarian-language translation of the

Bible, entirely from the Hebrew text, was its publication, too. It has also published many other important works. Its Yearbooks are an important source for this present study.
7. Jewish Museum archives [henceforth J. M. arch.].
8. Ibid.
9. Ibid.
10. J. M. arch. 81.189.
11. J. M. arch. 81.272.
12. IMIT Yearbook, 1912. 381.
13. J. M. arch. 81.321.
14. J.M. arch, 80.45; IMIT Yearbook, 1915. 408–435; IMIT Yearbook, 1916. 391–428.
15. IMIT Yearbook, 1916. 372–374.
16. J. M. arch. 80.60.
17. J. M. arch. 76.240.
18. IMIT Yearbook, 1929. 351–352.
19. Lajos Szabolcsi, son of Miksa Szabolcsi, author, journalist, succeeded his father as editor of *Egyenlőség*.
20. J. M. arch. 80.60.1.
21. IMIT Yearbook, 1931. 319.
22. J. M. arch. 80.124.
23. IMIT Yearbook, 1931. 324-326.

24. IMIT Yearbook, 1931. 326.
25. Adolf Wertheimer, bank director, art collector, IMIT president.
26. Ernő Munkácsi, lawyer. Active in various functions of the Israelite Congregation of Pest.
27. J. M. arch. 81.294.
28. IMIT Yearbook, 1933. 280–282.
29. IMIT Yearbook, 1933, 283–294. Ödön Gerő, art critic, publicist, member of boards of many art societies. Izsák Perlmutter, painter; his work was shown in many exhibitions.
30. Simon Hevesi, theologian, rabbi of the Israelite Congregation of Pest and later its Chief Rabbi, professor at the National Rabbinical Seminary, one of the founders of the National Hungarian Israelite Cultural Association.
31. IMIT Yearbook, 1933, 298–299.
32. IMIT Yearbook, 1933, 321–332.
33. IMIT Yearbook, 1933, 306.
34. IMIT Yearbook, 1933, 306–308.
35. IMIT Yearbook, 1933, 311–312.
36. OMIKE was established in 1908 with important cultural and charity functions. It maintained the Mensa Academica [student refectory] for Jewish academicians. In later years, it also ran a kollégium. It helped Jewish apprentices and children in poor financial circumstances. It maintained a library for Jewish students in schools of higher learning, organized courses for art students in painting and sculpting. An important activity of OMIKE was its theater program, which provided opportunities for authors, actors, musicians driven from their platforms and their stages by Fascism to make a living.
37. J. M. arch. 80.60; Libanon III (1938), No. 2. 64.
38. Libanon VII (1942), No. 3. 72–76; J. M. arch. 82.126.
39. J. M. arch. 80.82.
40. J. M. arch. 82.126.
41. J. M. arch. 81.215.
42. J. M. arch. 83.5, 80.6.
43. J. M. arch. 80.71.
44. AJDC, better known as JOINT, a great international charitable organization.
45. J. M. arch. 81.318.
46. György Kecskeméti: "Újra megnyitják az Országos Magyar Zsidó Múzeumot" [The National Hungarian Jewish Museum is Reopened], Új Élet III (1947), No. 27, 6.
47. Új Élet III [1947], No. 28, 9.
48. J. M. arch. 82.22.
49. Új Élet V [1949], No. 40, 12.
50. On November 9, 1938, almost all synagogues on German territory were burned down. The night of conflagration was named Kristallnacht, after the sparkling broken glass of the ruins that covered the streets.
51. József Katona: A 90 éves Dohány utcai templom [The 90-Year-Old Dohány Street Temple]; Fülöp Grünvald —Ernő Naményi: Budapesti zsinagógák [Synagogues in Budapest]. Published by the National Hungarian Jewish Museum, Budapest, 1949.
52. Új Élet V [1949], No. 15, 7.
53. The approximately quarter-million manuscript fragments accumulated in the Cairo synagogue.

CEREMONIAL OBJECTS

The Jewish Museum's collection of Judaica came into being largely through bequests, gifts and purchases. Only a small part is the result of purposeful collecting. The religious, synagogue and privately owned ritual objects, perhaps a couple of thousand in number,—the bulk of which is to be classified as applied art, as it is mainly metalwork—mirror Hungarian Jewry's centuries-old history, full of vicissitude, yet not wanting in luster and wealth.

The Jews appeared on the country's territory already in the 3rd century in what was Pannonia in the Roman period. The headstones also mention a synagogue around Intercisa (today's Dunaújváros).[1] But its remains have been destroyed by the storms of history just as those of the synagogues that were built in later centuries which are recalled in written data.

Jews settled in Buda after the Mongol invasion, in the 1250s. King Béla IV gave them that privilege in 1251 which, among others, assured the right of maintaining a synagogue. An important role was played in the issuance of the patent of privilege by the king's chamberlain, Comes Henel who, with his sons also rented the queen's tax collection and, in 1250, was bailiff of the mint in Esztergom.

He moved from Vienna to Hungary between 1246 and 1250. With his family, he established the first Jewish quarters in Buda. No trace is left of his wealth for which he was famous, nor of the furnishings of the first synagogue mentioned by the *Chronicle of Buda* in connection with an occurrence in 1302.[2] From 1364, the Jewish quarters were located on the north- and southwest side of what is today Táncsics Mihály utca. This is where they lived till the Turks were driven from Hungary (1686),[3] with the exception of the short period of the time between the Mohács Disaster and the fall of Buda (1526–1541). In this area stood their two synagogues, one of which was destroyed when the Turks were put to rout.[4] The Buda congregation reached the pinnacle of its development in the 15th and 16th centuries, lasting from King Matthias's ascent to the throne to the fall of Buda.

The wealthy and respected leaders of the congregation displayed a great deal of splendor at crownings and other festivities. Historians noted that King Matthias, on his way to be crowned in Székesfehérvár in 1464, was followed by a splendid group of Jews from Buda. A member of the famed and rich Mendel family was riding with 16 shield-bearers in front of the king. The retainer carrying the flag was followed by two pages "whose silver swords were attached to their waist by a rich and superb belt. These were followed by Mendel sword in hand and his company in his footsteps . . ."[5] In 1476, at Matthias's wedding procession, the Jews welcomed the king and his wife, Beatrice of Aragon, at the gates of the city. In the saddle, in full dress, their elder marched with 32 riders dressed in silver, in his hand a drawn sword, the basket of its grip being filled with ten pounds of silver. Behind him rode his son, also with a sword that had a grip's basket filled with silver. After them came 24 knights dressed in scarlet, finally, the procession closed with 200 turbaned Jews carrying a red flag with Hebrew inscription, embellished with a Star of David under which were three gold stars and above an embroidered gold crown. The elders stood under a canopy, amongst them one holding a gold-decorated Torah in his hand.[6] When Władisław II (1490–1516) entered the city, he, too, was greeted with a Torah.[7]

King Matthias heaped his court Jews, the esteemed Mendel family of Buda, with favors by appointing them to be permanent leaders of Hungary's Jewish community. The Mendels represented their country's Jews in a manner that fit their rank and wealth. On festive occasions, their appearance was admired by all. The Prefect moved about in Władisław II's wedding procession as the "Prince of the Jews". The Jews of Buda, who had extensive western contacts—especially members of the Mendel family and Imre Fortunatus, King Władisław's treasurer—must have used high standards in furnishing their synagogue. This is shown by the remains of the—even by Central European standards outstanding—late Gothic synagogue excavated in a parcel of land once owned by the Mendel family in the heart of the Jewish quarter. However, no trace is left of their wealth, though historical documents witness the fact that, on the liberation of Buda, the Emperor's men took 35 Torah scrolls of the congregation to Nikolsburg.[8]

The Jewish Museum's oldest ceremonial objects are a couple of pieces of Turkish workmanship made during the period of Turkish occupation (No. 20). They are a simple pair of copper Rimmonim whose upper part is in the form of a pomegranate and the engraved ornament is also pomegranate. According to the inscription, they were made by Tzvi Hersh, son of David in 1602.

The Rimmon (finial) is the oldest Torah ornament. The Hebrew name means pomegranate, which is the symbol of life and fertility in the East. In the Bible, it ornamented the High Priest's robe. It is put on the top of the Torah roller which is called Etz Hayyim, tree of life. The oldest Rimmon, dating from the 15th century, is preserved in the cathedral of Palma de Mallorca. The form of the Rimmon developed differently in countries of the East and the West. To the present, the typical Rimmon of the Near East has a comparatively small head on a cylindrical stem whereas in the West, it takes on the form of architecture and is shaped like a filigree turret. Variations with little bells that jingle when the Torah is carried around came into being in the 18th century. The most artistic ritual object of the Jewish Museum—made around 1700 according to its engraving—is a pair of Rimmonim donated by Abraham Sopher in 1701 (No.19). Its mark indicates that it was made by silversmith Angiello Scarbello d'Este of Padua. It was in Italy where the most exquisite Rimmonim were made. In shaping them, the silversmith took advantage of all of his artistic and technical talents. Both the form and the technical execution of these masterpieces, whose corresponding example is in the Israel Museum in Jerusalem, are admirable. The three-tiered Rimmonim are outstanding creations of European silversmiths. This is because of their detailed fine miniature work, the baroque utilization of light and shade effect, as well as their variations of interlocking curved decorations, and the little compartments opening on latticed balconies containing small gilt and cast figures of the Jerusalem sanctuary in them. The Budapest exemplars were executed more lavishly than those in Jerusalem; they also have ornaments hanging in two rows from the bottom.

Until most recent times, the Hungarian Jewish community has had close family, commercial, financial and cultural relations with Austria and Germany. Thus it is obvious that the rest of the Museum's Rimmonim —with the exception of the Krivoi Rog ivory Rimmon (No. 30)—would belong to the Austrian branch of Central European silversmith work. They are simple in form, their cylindrical stem is engraved with leaf-decoration in a style characteristic of the period, with rather large open crowns on top and bells inside them. Many of them are the work of Viennese masters. They show little variations which, at the same time, is a sign of Jewish traditionalism. They are usually topped by the double-headed heraldic eagle or the two tablets of the Ten Commandments. The pair of Rimmonim made by Viennese craftsman K.I. in 1818 which look like palm trees with bells among the branches, are of special interest (No. 27).

From the middle of the 18th century, the number of historical objects grow in number. The pair of Rimmonim of the congregation of Pest was made in 1754 by the Viennese silversmith Joseph Böheim (No. 21). It probably became the property of the congregation only later, since at the time there was as yet no congregation in Pest. The city had not permitted Jews to come into its territory for a hundred years after the Turks were driven out. Thus, the establishment of the congregation can be dated only from 1787.

The congregation in Buda, in constant struggle with the city's council after the liberation from the Turks, merely vegetated. In 1746, it was finally driven out altogether. Many of the exiled families moved to Óbuda, which was flourishing under the protection of the wife of Count Péter Zichy.

The Jews moved into Óbuda during the first decade of the 18th century. By the time of the 1737 census, 43 families had settled there. Their synagogue is first mentioned in 1738.[9] Ábrahám Trebitsch wrote about them in 1746 that they were a big congregation, "full of sages, rich and wealthy people."[10] Beside commerce, they were also engaged in trade, and there were craftsmen among them, too.

The Jewish Museum's 17th-century cup (No. 2) probably belonged to the first synagogue's utensils. There are three circles engraved on its side with garlanded heads of antique warriors in them and the inscription that the cup had been made at the order of the Óbuda Holy Society in 1749 (in which case, it must have been acquired that year). This simple, in that period widely used drinking cup is clear illustration of the fact that utensils, cup beakers, sugarbowls, originally made for secular use, became, with the passage of time, Jewish cultic objects. This change in function can be found all over Europe, not only among Jews but also in other denominations, for instance, among Protestants. This is also applicable to the early 17th-century Hungarian so-called fleece cup—also one of the Jewish Museum's silver objects (No. 1). The Museum has quite a collection of excellent work by European silversmiths consisting of silver goblets and cups originally secular in nature and later used for ritual purposes.

The Ashkenazi (German Jewish) tradition puts a Torah crown (*Keter*) or Rimmon (finial) on top of the *Etz Hayyim*, whereas the Sephardi (Spanish and Portuguese) sometimes puts a helmet there. In the northern countries, it used to be the custom through the centuries to have a Torah helmet on the Sabbath and the crown on all other holidays. This custom, however, sank into oblivion at the end of the last century.

Crowns have been known since the early Middle Ages, but the ones still in existence are mostly from the 17th century. Decoration of the crown is a floriate design recalling that the Torah was at first encircled by garlands. Apart from this, one can also find birds, animals (like lions, deer, eagles, leopards), and bells. The more elaborate ones are also decorated with gemstones.

The six arches of the oldest, partially gilt silver Torah crown in the possession of the Jewish Museum in Budapest are six prancing lions facing each other (*No. 31*). It was made in Cracow in the middle of the 18th century. There are other pieces known that are similar, such as the ones at the Israel Museum in Jerusalem and the one in the possession of the Jewish congregation of Cracow. The Torah crown of the Kugel collection in Paris—more elaborate than the one in Budapest—indicates Viennese origin.[11] The rest of the Torah crowns in the Budapest Museum were made either in Vienna or in Pest-Buda. Given the place of their period, they are of the Austrian and German closed crown type.

Starting in the second half of the 18th century and especially in the 19th, as the Pest-Buda Jews assumed a leading role, the Hungarian Jewish community provided the country's silversmiths and those of Pest-Buda with their orders. More than once, they created their greatest work for the synagogues—as, for instance, did János Mihály Schwager of Pest and János Mihály Müller for the synagogue in Óbuda. Though unique, they resemble each other. These Torah crowns are topped by a pair of Rimmonim. The resemblance of the two shows the expressed preference of the person who commissioned the second crown. The earlier one—though the inscription would suggest a later time—is the 1774 creation of János Mihály Schwager (*No. 34*). There are two twisted rods on the hoop that is decorated with a row of palmettes chased and embossed with acanthus leaves. The Rimmonim are attached to the palmettes by little twisted columns surrounded by an arched baroque grill on which little bells are hung. János Mihály Schwager (who probably worked between 1760 and 1791) was the firm's assay master providing a hallmark at the time when the Rimmonim were made.[12] He was among the guild's most accomplished craftsmen in Pest. The standard of his art of embossing was on a specially high level. Rococo and Louis XVI decoration interchange in his work. On the Torah ornament of the congregation in Óbuda and on the breastplate that belongs to it, made in 1779, the Louis XVI style already dominates in a milder form (*No. 37*). The breastplate has four columns, two bunches of fruit, a row of pearls and a canopy.

One and a half decades later, János Mihály Müller, who was active in Pest from 1781,[13] adopted Schwager's style of form and ornamentation. He put two rows of beads at the bottom of the loop of the coronet, but in the upper, ornamental part, the softer bending rococo curved arches return (*No. 35*).

According to Ashkenazi tradition, a breastplate is hung by chain on the Torah mantle which is part of the Torah decorations. The Sephardim do not know this custom. The earliest known breastplates are from the beginning of the 17th century. They have a square opening in the middle for the insertion of a little plate showing the holiday. They are reminiscent of the breastplate worn by the High Priest. This was decorated with twelve precious stones symbolic of the twelve tribes of Israel. This may be the reason for the use of colored stones for breastplates. The form of the breastplate has changed in the course of centuries in accordance with the style of the given period. The earliest are square, the later ones are either half round or oval on top. Their technique varies, they are embossed, chased and occasionally filigree work. Beside the floral decoration that is characteristic of a period's fashion, they show Jewish symbols as well, mostly the tablets of the Ten Commandments, heraldic lions, the Lion of Judah holding the Torah crown, deer, and two twisted columns representing the Yahin and Boaz pillars of the destroyed Temple in Jerusalem. However, human shapes also appear in the figures of Moses and Aaron.

The Jewish Museum in Budapest has a rich collection of such Torah breastplates. The earliest one is the breastplate of the Hevrah Kaddishah of Pest. It is the 1754 work of Joseph Böheim (*No. 36*). Its shape is that of the Holy Ark, a rampant lion on the twisted column at each side, and a coronet on top. The majority of the Museum's breastplates is the work of Viennese craftsmen. Most of them were made at the beginning of the 19th century when the fortunes of Pest-Buda's Jews rose in leaps and bounds. Two have the figures of Moses and Aaron with the two tablets between them under a canopy (*Nos. 39, 40*); four have rampant lions and on three, the lions stand on columns (*Nos. 41, 43, 44*). This had become the dominant form until the middle of the 19th century because Pál Cseh (mentioned : 1854–1868),[14] gold and silversmith, had made his own neo-baroque rocaille ornamented breastplate, probably on commission, in this way. It has a rampant lion on each side holding a crown above the tablets of the Ten Commandments (*No. 43*).

The partially gilt silver, wholly filigree, lace-edged Torah breastplate (No. 38) is special. It has in the middle between two columns an arch-topped little cabinet with the Tablets of the Law in it. Above this is an oriental-looking big open crown topped by an orb that ends in a point. The same decoration is also found on top of the columns. The turquois stones, too, indicate oriental, perhaps Balkan origin. The Hebrew date on it corresponds to 1770, but the object is probably older. It may have come from the end of the Turkish occupation (late 17th century).

The Torah scroll must not be touched with the naked hand. A pointer (Yad) is used. The Hebrew word means hand. The pointer ends in an outstretched right hand with the index finger pointing. It is hung on a long chain on the Torah mantle. It was not yet known in the Middle Ages. Sources mention it starting in the 16th century. As a rule, it is made of silver, but the Museum in Budapest displays one, made at the end of the 19th century, a Transylvanian pointer whittled of wood, as an ethnic curiosity (No. 49). The handle of the pointer changes with the style. Sometimes it is round, at others, square. Its stem is cylindrical, it can be twisted or square, may have precious stones in it and, occasionally, it may be enameled.

The Prague Torah pointer, made in the first half of the 19th century with the TH trademark, represents the simpler, conventional Central European style with its twisted stem topped by the pointing finger (No. 45). The square stemmed Torah pointer (No. 48) made by Fülöp Adler[15] is a well-balanced piece. (More is said about his work in connection with the silversmiths of Óbuda.) Also well-balanced work is the square stemmed pointer (No. 46) made in 1834 by the leading master craftsman of the guild of the silversmiths in Buda, József Károly Gretschl, Sr. (1799–1886).[16] This master had done much work for the Jewish congregation in the capital. Many of his creations are included in the exhibits.

The pitchers and bowls are used for the symbolic washing of hands before the priestly blessing of the Cohen. Their form does not differ from that used for secular purposes. Most of the time, it is the Hebrew inscription only—when the utensil is made to order—that indicates its ritual use. Often the signs of the Cohen can be seen on them. Sets of lavers belonging to the poorer congregations are pewter, the rest are of silver.

The small tinned copper mug of the Jewish Museum in Budapest is simple. It was possibly made by a Hungarian village craftsman in the 18th century (No. 50).

The pewter can with the Hebrew inscription giving the date 1834 on it and its deep bowl are already more ambitious Hungarian workmanship of the middle of the 18th century. Though secular in nature, the inscription's date shows that they were later used for ritual purposes (Nos. 51, 52). Extraordinarily beautiful is the 1757 pitcher of the Levi made by the Viennese Frantz Lintzberger (No. 53). The cracker-biscuit-shaped bowl with PD initials is also the creation of a Viennese master. It was given to the Hevrah Kaddishah in Pest almost a hundred years later, in 1845 (No. 54).

An outstanding example of Hungarian craftsmanship is the Levi's pitcher made in 1797 by József Prandtner, Sr.,[17] the most important silversmith of late 18th century Pest (No. 55). (The Levi is a descendant of the Biblical tribe of Levi. The Levites symbolically wash the hands of the Cohen before he blesses the congregation.) This had a bowl, too, which disappeared after 1935. That bowl's rim was decorated by the same garlanded, tiny flowered pattern as the neck, base and body of the elegant pitcher. The lower part of the pitcher has embossed spear-shaped leaves for decoration, the mouth is beaded, and the handle is made in the shape of a serpent. The antique-inspired Empire-style form and lively lines are a testimony to the fine art of Central European silversmiths.

More modest, yet well proportioned, is the Cohen's pitcher ordered for Cohenite function by the Hevrah Kaddishah in Pest in 1824 (No. 56). It was made also by a craftsman in Pest, Ferenc Schmidt (worked 1820–1865).[18] On the body, in front, is the embossed symbol of the Cohen.

The rich series of beakers, cups and glasses (Kiddush cups are used for blessing over wine on the Sabbath and festivals) in the possession of the Museum embraces the period from the end of the 17th century to the present day. The majority comes from famous German silversmith centers (Augsburg, Nuremberg), but there are also Austrian, Hungarian, Polish and even Russian items. Often they were originally made for secular use but, according to their inscriptions, they were turned into ritual purposes. Many are the work of outstanding silversmiths, such as the "Bunch of Grapes" Goblet (No. 4) given to the Hevrah Kaddishah of Pest in 1836, the work of Georg Müller of Nuremberg (1624–1660), and the double-tiered high-embossed shell-ornamented beaker made by Hanss Reiff, also of Nuremberg (No. 5) who became a master silversmith in 1609. Further, the 17th-century beaker with cover from Augsburg whose cylindrical body is decorated by the embossed busts of Solon, Cyrus rex, and Pythagoras, each in a medal (No. 94), became a ritual object by having the blessing for Etrog engraved on it. The lidded cup decorated with acanthus leaf garlands belonging to the sick-visiting society of Kanizsa is the work of the HC-initiated master who worked in Salzburg (No. 9). Johann Wagner (1677–1725), the master silversmith of Augsburg, made the flower-embossed, silver, lidded cup (No. 13) belonging to the Hevrah Kaddishah of Pest. These cups with lid were originally meant for ceremonial purposes.

The bubbled cup decorated with the ten plagues in Egypt (No. 14) was made for ritual purposes in the 18th century, and so was the niello enameled, typically Russian technique cup (No. 15) made in Moscow in 1804 with scenes of the life of Moses. A simple drinking goblet is the memorial cup of Lipót Lőw, Chief Rabbi of Nagykanizsa (No. 16), and so is the 1851 chalice of the Hevrah Kaddishah in Óbuda which was embossed by József Gretschl, Jr. (No. 17). With its vertical ribbing, it represents characteristic neo-baroque form. Modern Hungarian silversmith work is represented by Margit Tevan's (1908–1978) "Elijah Cup" of 1937 with cover. The cup illustrates the Bauhaus lines characteristic of the artist's style (No. 18).

Charity boxes are usually made for the Bikkur Holim (Society in Aid of the Poor and Sick) and Hevrah Kaddishah (Holy Society that deals with the dead and funerals) to assist relatives of the sick and the dead. The Jewish Museum has many charity plates and boxes which once were among the accessories of the former synagogue in Óbuda. The oldest, which according to its Hebrew inscription was commissioned in 1758 by David's daughter, the goodwife Pearl, spouse of the synagogue's president, is lost.[19] However, the simple, half-round, horizontally edged little collection plate that had been ordered by the Gabbaim (wardens of the synagogue) of the Óbuda Hevrah Kaddishah in 1786 (according to minor count of years—omitting the thousands, 546, anno mundi), is still in existence. Presumably, it is the work of a Jewish silversmith.

Óbuda played a significant part in the history of the work of Jewish silversmiths. All over Hungary, the guilds had not admitted Jews into their organizations until the beginning of the 19th century. In Óbuda, however, they had the privilege of pursuing their trade. Although as a rule Jews had been engaged in commerce and finance, the 18th-century census lists some craftsmen among them—thus, goldsmiths, too.[20] In 1749, when the Jews of Pozsony petitioned Queen Maria Theresa to respond to their grievances, one of their requests was to permit Jewish craftsmen and traders to pursue their professions freely and unhindered at their place of residence. The Queen referred their complaints to the Council of the Governor-General.[21] In Óbuda, however, they were free to work under Countess Erzsébet Zichy's—and from 1766—the Cabinet's protection.

Israel Marcus was the Zichy family's silversmith. He made a pair of silver spurs for Count Miklós Zichy in 1755. The Pest County census of 1767 mentions three goldsmiths in Óbuda : Israel Marcus, Leebl Goldsmit and Salamon Véér. The 1803 census mentions also the guild of the goldsmiths. These craftsmen in Óbuda and those with homes in Pozsonyvártelek already had their own hallmark at the end of the 18th century. This could be seen on the silver cup of 1815 that was part of the Óbuda synagogue equipment, now lost. According to its inscription, it was the gift of Moshe Tzoref (silversmith) and his wife to the Hevrah.[22] Starting with the beginning of the 19th century, the number of Jewish goldsmiths increased.

They made simple, mainly ritual objects like the small collection plate of the synagogue in Óbuda, mentioned earlier, Torah pointers, and the frame and handle of the thin little silver tablet used by the synagogue of Óbuda to give to the person called to read from the Torah. (Its inscription indicates that it was made in 1781.) The characteristic technique was to manipulate thin silver wire into filigree work. Starting with the last decades of the 18th century, they used this technique for small synagogue utensils, spiceboxes, baptismal medals, buttons of Hungarian gala dresses, buckles, and pipe bowls. Filigree technique, which was very popular in the Near East, was revived after the Middle Ages in the South German silversmith centers at the end of the 17th century. This was so especially in Munich, in Schwäbisch-Gmünden. Through the instrumentality of Austrian and Jewish traders, it soon spread to Hungary too, and from the end of the 18th century, it flourished in Bohemia, Poland and the Ukraine.

Filigree work usually takes the form of vegetation, but occasionally, it was also made into figures like the heraldic eagle. Filigreed objects can also be found among the art treasures of the Prague ghetto. This was the preferred technique of Óbuda craftsmen, too. However, the silversmiths of Pest and Buda also employed it when making ceremonial objects for their Jewish customers. The Jewish Museum's 18th-century partially gilt filigreed silver pair of Rimmonim with leaf-ornamented crowns topped by a pressed bell is probably the work of a Jewish silversmith (No. 29). The Polish Rimmon, made in the middle of the 18th century, part of the Parisian Kugel Collection and shown at the Frankfurt Synagogue Exhibition, likewise has a ball-shaped crown on top of its cylindrical stem.[23]

The activities of József Polák as a silversmith can be traced back to 1820. In that year, he made a five-piece collection of filigreed Torah accessories. We also know of his filigreed little basket (Historical Museum, Budapest) and frames for medals used in baptismal ceremonies (Hungarian National Museum). Sámuel Engel, whose activities can be traced to 1820, was also engaged in filigree work.[24] Fülöp Adler, whose existing pieces demonstrate that he started his activities in 1825, had also done filigree work. (We have already mentioned him in connection with his Torah pointer of 1836.)

However, the congregation in Óbuda made its purchases both from native and foreign silversmiths indiscriminately. In 1802, they obtained from the silversmith Antal Müller (1789–1815)[25] a charity plate (No. 57). In 1815, the master silversmith Pál Czigler (1769–1824)[26] made a similar charity plate (No. 58) for them. It was purchased by the trustees with the money provided by Itzig Totis's house of prayer. The congregation was loyal to this form, for in 1859 they ordered a similar bowl (No. 67) from master silversmith Pál Cseh of Pest. This style is varied in a more elegant way in the bowl with stand that has three divisions in its center (No. 61), made by József Károly Gretschl, Sr. mentioned above. Ferenc Pasperger (1775–1834),[27] Chief Master of the guild in Pest, made an elegant Empire-style charity box (No. 60) in 1882 for the Hevrah Kaddishah in Óbuda. It has a big molded lion on the lid, and the handle has the shape of a snake. The oblong collection box (No. 65) ordered from the Viennese silversmith Corn Sagg von Sach by the congregation in Nagykanizsa, has a unique style. It has two twisted columns in front from which hangs the Eternal Light. The covered charity box of the Hevrah in Nagykanizsa (No. 64) was made by the Viennese T. Mayerhoffer in 1848. The neo-baroque, richly embossed, rocaille flowered charity box (No. 63) was made by Ferenc Schmidt in 1855.

The spicebox, the Jewish ritual object which has always been made with the most imagination, is the ever present requisite of the Havdallah ceremony. A Havdallah (leave-taking of the Sabbath) ceremony's integral part is the pleasant-smelling mixture of spices, of myrtle, cinnamon, etc., kept in a receptacle (Bessamim) made for the purpose. The usage refers to verse 5:13 in the Song of Songs, "His cheeks are as a bed of spices. As towers of sweet herbs." The spicebox is usually silver, but can also be made of tin, copper and wood. The use of spices was already known in the first century; however, the form of the spicebox developed among the Ashkenazi Jews in Germany during the Middle Ages. There is a literary source for the fact that one of the most famous rabbis of the 15th century, Israel Isserlein (1390–1460) of Regensburg, had already one in his household, and the Italian David Reubeni had, in 1536, two made of silver.[28] The earliest pieces look like turrets. This traditional and most frequent form, with its filigree balcony on its floors, windows that can be opened, flag on top and some even with clocks and watchmen, is reminiscent of the look-out tower of the Middle Ages. The spiceboxes of the late Middle Ages even imitate the masonry of the walls. Such a spicebox is illustrated in a German liturgical book of 1590.[29] The earliest examples in existence, dating from the middle of the 16th century, are from Germany. Their use became general in the 19th century in Ashkenazi Jewish households. Attachment of Jewish ritual art to tradition has preserved the ancient form; what's more, today it recreates it. The Jewish Museum in Budapest has a whole series of turret-shaped spiceboxes. The oldest is the one with Nuremberg hallmark made at the end of the 17th century (No. 69). Many of the pieces are East-European filigree work of the 18th century, but there are some among them which, when compared with other products of silversmiths in Óbuda as, for example, the little two-storied tower standing on human feet with a bell in it and a flag on top (No. 73), may be considered the work of Jewish silversmiths of Óbuda.

The older type of 18th-century turret-shape spiceboxes is represented by the single-story spicebox with catwalk and clock, looking like a brick building. It has GG for monogram and was made in Nuremberg (No. 76). The spicebox with checkered cylindrical body imitating masonry work and embossed horizontal leaf collar on its stem may also be the product of the late 18th century (No. 75).

The spiceboxes made in Pest-Buda are also unique. Outstanding among them is the one with specially beautiful filigree work. According to its hallmark letter, it was made between 1806 and 1810. The two stories rest on a square stand, the spire is bent like a dome and ends in a ball and flag (No. 77). It was made by Vilmos (Wilhelm) Meitinsky[30] (perhaps Jewish), a non-guild member, or Vince Messerschmied, a silversmith in Pest. Its general plan and especially the formation of its filigree work are like those of the spicebox shown at the exhibition organized by the Israel Museum, Jerusalem, in 1982. According to its hallmark letter, it was also made between 1806 and 1810 by Ferenc Máthé, silversmith in Pest.[31] (It belongs to the Hanfield Collection.) To this date, research knows only of smaller pieces of Ferenc Máthé's work from around 1800: his coat-chain and set of buttons. Similar to these is the foliate, fruit and flower-decorated, turret-shaped spicebox on four palmette legs and topped by a filigree ball (No. 72). It was made in the Gretschl workshop in the middle of the 19th century. Entirely differently made is the turret-shaped spicebox (No. 79) standing on a square decorated with semicircles formed by numbers of eight. It has no balcony. The hallmark 13 stamped into it would indicate that it was made in Hungary in the first half of the

19th century. The form of object No. 34 shown at the quoted Jerusalem exhibition is similar and might also be Hungarian.

The Museum's most detailed spicebox (No. 81) was made for the Kanizsa congregation, probably in Hungary, in 1831. Its garlands are formed of little circles, it is slender in form, turret-shaped, enriched by a cameo and colored glass. Its square, tall stand follows 18th-century style. This form also served as the basis of the work of silversmith Ignác Cserekviczky, mentioned 1854–1868 (No. 82).

According to its customs stamp, the Museum's three-storied filigree turret spicebox with a deer-shaped little flag and a man blowing a Shofar on its round top (No. 80) was probably made in Vienna. At the quoted Jerusalem exhibition, there was a replica of this spicebox from the Wiesbaden Collection.

The three-tiered turret spicebox on tall stand with dome-like top (No. 74) was made in Eastern Europe, perhaps in Poland, in the 19th century. So was the small round utensil on a tall stand and eight-lobed foot (No. 78). This form points to Poland and Eastern Europe, where naturalistic fruit-form worked in miniature was much favored. Such a pear-shaped artistic piece with a lion on its stem reaching for the branch of a fruit tree (No. 71) was made in Cracow around 1830. The above-mentioned Jerusalem exhibition showed similar Polish pieces of simpler design.

Of special interest among the Museum's variety of naturalistic spiceboxes are the tiny cow (No. 88) and locomotive (No. 89) of the second half of the 19th century. They are possibly Hungarian made, the former from Pest-Buda, the latter from Óbuda. The small locomotive's corresponding piece, including a little fish with movable parts, was present at the spicebox exhibition in Jerusalem. The collection in Budapest also has such a little fish (No. 84) which, according to its hallmark, was made in Paris in 1809 or 1810.

The filigree work little box in the shape of a prayerbook (No. 86) is a lovely piece. It is probably the work of a Hungarian craftsman, also of the 19th century.

The little dove box (No. 83) may have been made in Hungary or in Vienna, whereas the slender cast copper filigree gondola (No. 87) is Upper Italian—perhaps Venetian—work from the 19th century.

The candle snuffer shaped boxes with delicately worked tray embossed with curved leaves were originally not meant to be used for spices. Both were made in Vienna in 1836 (No. 85).

The Jewish New Year (Rosh Hashanah) is a festival of introspection, soul searching and repentance. During prayers, the congregation is called to repentance by sounding of the Shofar, a trumpet made of ram's horn. The animal's horn is bent into traditional shape. As a rule, it is entirely unadorned, only the ends are notched. Occasionally, Hebrew inscription may be found on it. The period of repentance is culminated by the Day of Atonement, Yom Kippur, Judaism's holiest day. Again, the Shofar is sounded. This is reminiscent of the sacrifice of Isaac and it proclaims forgiveness of sins.

The Museum's Shofar of black bent horn is very simple, decorated only with rings carved into it which divide it (No. 90). It was probably made at the beginning of the 19th century and comes from Tunisia.

On New Year's Day, the head of the family offers a slice of apple dipped in honey to members of the family. Some families use a special honeypot or tray for the purpose. The Jewish Museum in Budapest has a porcelain honeypot with cover (No. 91) on exhibit, made in the middle of the 19th century in the Bohemian Giesshübl factory. According to the painted inscription, it was made specially for this purpose.

The traditional garb of the holidays is a white linen Kittel—a gown held together at the waist by a belt and buckle. The Museum's Viennese embossed silver buckle from the 19th century (No. 92) has a Torah crown and two heraldic lions—the Lions of Judah—on it. Often, these buckles show the sacrifice of Isaac.

Verse 16:23 in Exodus prescribes the first harvest festival. Succoth is one of the three great Pilgrimage Festivals. The 23rd Chapter of the Book of Leviticus calls upon Jews to dwell in booths of leafy boughs ("in booths shall you dwell for seven days"). The Etrog and Lulav stand as symbols of the booths. The Etrog —the citrus fruit—is kept in a vessel made for the purpose. This vessel, as is appropriate, is often shaped like a citrus fruit. The Lulav is a palm branch, to it are added myrtle and weeping willow. Accordingly, these leaves frequently appear on ritual objects.

The German pewter plate of the 19th century with its wavy rim and molded scene of the holiday in the middle (No. 93) was made for Tabernacles.

One of the most beautiful and oldest pieces of the collection is the Etrog container that was originally owned by the former Bikkur Holim Society. Actually, it was made by a Hungarian silversmith of Transylvania in the 17th century and was meant to be a jewelry tray (No. 95). The other two Etrog containers had also been made for secular purposes. One is a covered sugar bowl made by the Viennese I. A. Kölbel in 1744 (No. 96) and the other, showing a mythological scene, was made in Buda in the already mentioned workshop of Gretschl in 1833 (No. 97).

The silver coconut chalice with engraved scenes, inscribed with the blessing for taking the Lulav, comes from Kiev (No. 98).

On 25 Kislev starts the eight-day Hanukkah festival, the Festival of Lights, commemorating the rededication of the Temple in Jerusalem. That is when the legendary miracle of the sacred oil in the Temple is recalled—how it lasted for eight days after the cleansing of the Temple in Jerusalem (B. Talmud, Shabbat 21b). The highlight of the Hanukkah festival is the lighting of the wicks of the Hanukkah candelabrum each evening. At the same time, the eight little lights are the symbol of the holy flame of faith. The candelabrum has a ninth light, too, the so-called shamash, used to light the others. The Eastern European, chiefly the Polish, Hanukkah lamp often displays two of them, always a little higher than the other eight.

The Hanukkah lamp is originally a domestic ritual object, examples of which have survived from the Roman era. The kind that has a bench developed in the Middle Ages. This is the most frequent type even today. In front of the back, which is higher, is the row of wick-holders and, on the side, somewhat higher, is the shamash. The back, as is demonstrated by the remaining examples, used to be triangular during the Renaissance and the Middle Ages. Responding to changes in style, however, its contour changed in the course of later centuries, becoming lighter, voluted and scrolled. Its form often resembles a synagogue. The majority of Hanukkah lamps are made of brass or bronze, but some are of pewter and iron. The more expensive ones are silver. The evolution of their shapes shows many variations by country, strongly influenced by the artistic talent and technical knowledge of the master craftsmen who made them.

Sources of the Middle Ages tell us about Hanukkah lights set up in synagogues for the travelers and the poor who were unable to light them at home. For this reason, these lamps had to be larger. This is how the form of the seven-branched candelabrum, the menorah of the destroyed Temple in Jerusalem, was revived. The Temple menorah is memorialized in many illustrations and, first of all, in Titus's arch of triumph in Rome. The oldest menorahs come to us from the 14th century. The seven-branched menorah is a symbol; the Hanukkah menorah is a ritual object and has eight plus one branches and eight plus one lights. The Hanukkah candelabrum was initially an oil lamp; of late, candles burn in it. It is often shaped like a symbolic tree, its branches on the two sides have leaves, buds and flowers as is described in the Book of Exodus (25:35). With the passage of time, the menorah-shaped candlestick, in smaller form, also found its way into the Jewish home.

The Jewish Museum in Budapest has a rich collection of Hanukkah lamps. The oldest one is Italian from the 16th century, antoher rather early one was originally the property of Chief Rabbi Koppel Reich of Pest. It is brass, in the shape of the Temple menorah (No. 99). It was made in the 17th century. It has a richly balustered stem. The big brass menorah, whose base is held by three pillars rising out of lions, was donated to the Holy Society of Lemberg by the goodwife Baile around 1700 (No. 100). Also of the middle of the 17th century, Polish made, is the very beautifully executed menorah (No.101) whose replica, owned by the Museum für Landschaft in Altona, was shown in 1961 at the Frankfurt Synagogue Exhibition.[32]

The back of 18th and 19th-century Hanukkah lamps are usually openwork decorated. Birds, eagles, deer and heraldic lions appear, placed symmetrically among the stylized garland. The bust of Emperor Joseph II (1780–1790), the issuer of the Tolerance Edict, appears on a copper Hanukkah lamp (No. 102). Another, Bohemian Hanukkah lamp of the Museum, is decorated with the bust of Napoleon (No. 105). The design of the cups in which the wicks are placed also varies. In the main, they are angular, but we find them even in the form of fish, as on the Museum's menorah on whose back are two deer, and two birds on top (No. 103). One variation of this type was shown at the Frankfurt Synagogue Exhibition.[33] The bronze and brass lamps are usually Polish made. In Poland, the Jewish foundry workers were highly skilled that, according to records, the candelabrum of the great synagogue of Dohány utca in Budapest had also been ordered from them. The primitive, eight-chairs Polish lead menorah made of bullets (No. 109) is no artistic masterpiece, but a moving testimony of faith in the East European 18th-century tradition. It comes down to us from World War I.

A beautiful example of silver Hanukkah lamps is the one made at the beginning of the 19th century in Poland. It has the shape of a synagogue and is richly decorated. It has a filigree back, the little oil lamps on its bench are shaped like pitchers, and a little bird stands on a big open crown on top (No. 108). A similar Hanukkah lamp was shown at the synagogue exhibition in Frankfurt. This one had two deer on its two filigree sides.[34] The collection closes with a high quality Hanukkah lamp made around 1830 in Austria or Hungary. The back has a canopy held up by angels, under it is an antique oil cruse surrounded by a vine tendril, symbolic of the cruse in the Jerusalem Temple (No. 110). Its little oil lamps are also special: they look like little baskets woven of rushes. The back is missing from the artistically executed Viennese piece. Unexpectedly, a peacock with its tail widely spread stretches its wings over the eight lion-shape oil lamps (No. 111).

Fülöp Adler made the fine Hanukkah lamp with the elegant lines (No. 112) in 1864 in Óbuda. Its beauty is created by its light composition—the filigree supports connected with a palmette decorated belt that holds the oil lamps and, in the middle, two swans holding a lyre in the Empire tradition.

In addition to lamps made for ritual purposes, Jewish households also had lamps for secular use. These were in accordance with the style of a given period as is illustrated by the two pairs of Viennese neo-baroque silver candlesticks from the middle of the 19th century (Nos. 113, 115).

On the festival of Purim, Jews celebrate their miraculous escape from death and memorialize their rescuers, Esther, wife of the Persian King Ahasuerus, and her uncle, Mordecai. The story is told in the Book of Esther which is read in public on this holiday. These scrolls (Megillah) are the masterpieces of Jewish miniature art. They are kept in leather, ivory or silver cases. They are popular gifts whose design has given the artists untold opportunities throughout the centuries to show their skills. The Museum's Viennese silver Megillah case from 1844 that can be opened has the traditional cylindrical form that was general in the 18th and 19th centuries. It has stylized leaf decoration, bubbles on both ends, and a pineapple knob (No. 114).

Purim is the holiday of joy and of distributing presents. The traditional food for Purim—the Purim loaf, fruit, etc.—is placed on trays used for the purpose. They are usually pewter. The Museum has a rich collection of these. With their decorations and inscriptions, they all refer to the holiday. Their decoration often includes figures from the Book of Esther. Mordecai's victory is illustrated most frequently, as can be seen on the Museum's pewter tray (No. 117) from the late 18th or the early 19th century. It has the quotation from the Book of Esther, "So Haman took the garb and the horse and arrayed Mordecai and paraded him through the city square . . ." (6:11). Since there were probably Jewish artisans among the pewter casters who worked outside the guilds, few of the trays are marked. The characters of the Hebrew inscriptions and the designs on some of the trays are identical, as on the Purim tray mentioned above, while the standard of the engraved Hebrew letters is high. We can therefore assume that they are the creations of Jewish craftsmen. The figures are often dressed in the garb of the period. For example, according to its inscription, the tray which had been the property of the synagogue in Baja personifies Haman as an insurrectionist captain of the 17th and 18th centuries (No. 116). The decoration is also frequently pseudo-folk, as for instance on the tray from Baja which has a stylized pomegranate and tulip garland.

Passover (Pessah), the Festival of Exodus from Egypt (11th century, B. C. E.), starts on the eve of the holiday with the Seder dinner, which has a special order prescribed by tradition. It is the Jewish housewife's responsibility to set the festive table of Seder night with the necessary table cloth, the utensils, the unleavened bread, and to prepare holiday dishes. The symbolic food is placed on a tray specially designated for the purpose, called the Seder plate. In front of every table setting stands a goblet of glass, silver or pewter as required by tradition, and in front of the head of the family is the most valuable cup of the house, the Cup of Elijah, the symbol of Messianic hope.

Generally, the Seder plates are pewter, but since the 17th and 18th centuries, they have also been made of majolica, earthenware and porcelain. Characteristic of all of them is the inscription of the order of the Seder, but pictures of figures can also be seen on them, usually those of the celebrating family. The Jewish Museum in Budapest owns an impressive collection of Seder plates. The popularity of Biblical scenes on such trays is shown by the fact that, from the end of the 18th century, in German-speaking places, they have also been made of silver.

Our series of ceramic Seder plates opens with the majolica tray of 1652 marked with the name of Jacob Azulai of Pesaro and Psalm 114 (No. 119). More examples of such trays with high coloring and crowded decoration are found in the Jewish museums of Prague, London and Paris. They were made in the workshops of Faenza, Padua, Mantua, Urbino and were from the 16th century to the 20th century. Because of the similarity of their patterns and pictures, the possibility cannot be excluded that they were copied on order. The Biblical scenes in cartouche frames are rather rough.

Judging by the inscriptions on majolica Seder plates, in the 17th and 18th centuries the families of Cohen and Azulai specialized themselves in their production. Their form and design follow the same pattern : there are four relief-contour cartouche-shape insets with floral decoration or Biblical figures (Moses, Aaron, David, Solomon), and four larger insets of Biblical and holiday scenes on the rim, like on the plate above. In the middle of the trays is the prayer, or the Kiddush, and Ha Lahma—the invitation to the table—in Hebrew letters. The trademark of the maker can be found on the bottom. A majolica tray of similar design in the Museum comes from Ancona. According to its inscription, it was made in 1654 by Jacob the Cohen (No. 118).

From the middle of the 18th century, in aristocratic households pewter was slowly being replaced by faience and porcelain, and by the end of the century, even ordinary households turned to the easily available, mass-produced earthenware trays. A few earthenware Seder plates of Hungarian manufacture from the beginning of the 19th century characteristic of the period can be found in the Jewish Museum in Budapest. These were made on order and can be distinguished from dishes of secular use only by what is painted on them as, for instance, the scalloped Seder plate decorated with the hand-painted picture of Marcus Benedictus (No. 120), or the plate with the somewhat naive illustration of the Wise Son (No. 123). Both come from the manufacture in Pápa and were made for the Fischer family.

The Fischer family played an important part in 19th-century Hungarian ceramics. Mór Fischer, a potter in Tata, founded the now world-famous Herend pottery in 1839, then just a modest earthenware factory. Prior to that date, he had rented a pottery in Pápa for two years between 1837 and 1839. After much difficulty, the as yet modest porcelain factory began to flourish in 1844. During the second half of the century, it developed a high artistic style of hand-painting with motifs of its own. It is still loyal to that standard, and it is thanks to this loyalty that it enjoys world-wide fame today.

The Jewish Museum's collection of Herend Seder plates plays an important part in the history of Hungarian ceramics, for it demonstrates the factory's development in the middle of the 19th century. The earliest piece is from the late 1830s. It is an oval earthenware dish (No. 125) with openwork, rosette-ornamented rim and quotes from the Seder ceremony in oval relief garlands. In the middle is the text of Ha Lahma in a rose garland, the typical Bohemian porcelain decoration of the period. Another plate is of porcelain. In the middle is a multicolored naturalistic Bohemian rose wreath worked carefully like a miniature (No. 122). In the petals of one of the roses we can already see the precursor of the Chinese influenced Victoria pattern of flowers that is so famous today. In the middle of a newer piece appears the local variation of the German Meissen bouquet of garden flowers, the Herend tulip pattern. However, the rim still has the characteristic Viennese "parsley" decoration with little daisies (No. 124). The rim of another tray has a basket-weave design still popular today, and in the middle is a highly artistic representation of a family as it celebrates Seder, done like a miniature (No. 126). This series, made in the middle of the last century, had been the order of an individual, probably a member of the Fischer family, the owners of the pottery. Such is the porcelain Seder goblet of Vilmos Farkasházy Fischer, son of Mór Fischer (No. 133). On this is the hand-painted portrait of his father in a gold frame. According to the inscription, it was painted in 1879 by Vilmos Fischer himself in Kolozsvár. The goblet, as far as its painted decoration is concerned, is not related to the Herend style, but follows the pattern of Bohemian porcelain of the period.

During his youth, Vilmos Fischer was responsible for directing the painting in his father's pottery in Herend. He therefore had a great part in the development of the typical Herend style. His spouse was Franciska, the daughter of Izrael Grünn, merchant in Marosújvár, and sugar manufacturer in Kolozsvár. His wife's parents did not want their daughter to go as far as Herend, so in 1874 Vilmos Fischer set up a painting works in Kolozsvár which was active until 1900. At first he painted on white Herend merchandise, later on Bohemian porcelain. His workshop flourished—he employed as many as eight or ten painters. He used mainly one variation of a pattern, a lavishly gilded, so-called Kubasch pattern. This is the way he painted the Seder plate with Ha Lahma in the middle (No. 129). There is a Kubasch pattern goblet of his in a private collection that has the miniature portraits of his father and mother painted in his own hand for their golden anniversary.[35] Also from Vilmos Fischer's workshop is the delicately painted Seder tray on stand made with geometrically arranged decoration (No. 128).

Hand-painting on porcelain became fashionable in the 1880s. In Hungary, the most notable workshops were in Budapest (the Láng workshop which popularized amateur painting, the Hüttl factory), in Herend (Anton's workshop), in Ungvár (the Industrial Technical School), in Modor, in Városlőd and in Pozsony (Jonas Fleischer). An item of interest in the history of ceramics is the activity of Jónás Neumann of Nyitra, two of whose painted Seder plates (Nos. 130, 131) are owned by the museum.

A proper representative of Hungarian Biedermeier is the simple but very functional tiered Seder tray made of wood with five cups on top to hold the symbolic food (No. 132). A significant example of polished Bohemian crystal of the 19th century is the Museum's cup (No. 134) with a Seder scene engraved on it. The simple wine flask with the Seder scenes was produced in Hungarian glassworks in 1860 (No. 135).

The pewter Seder plates come from the 18th and 19th centuries. The earliest is a Bohemian work of 1759. It has an artless heraldic griffin engraved in its center (No. 136). The beautifully contoured baroque tray marked "F. EVERS" is a typical dish used by the general public during the period (No. 138). The 18th-century, rather artistic item showing a Seder scene with the initials C. W. was probably made in Germany, or perhaps in the Tyrol (No. 139). The background represents an open hall with columns, and all mountains in the distance. Further research may discover the maker—possibly Hungarian—of the Seder plate with the pictures of David and Goliath and the engraved inscription, "Josephus Adler Anno 1829" on the bottom (No. 142). The naive charm of the figures, the decorative Hebrew letters of much higher quality would indicate that the Seder plate dated 1819 with a steeple flanked by two healdic lions on it (No. 141) was made by the same craftsman.

Jewish religious life is closely connected with the prayerbook. Just as tradition gives form to every manifestation of life, so it prescribes the order of prayers. Prayerbooks are always provided with valuable covers, they are bound in velvet, leather and, in well-to-do families, often in silver. The Jewish Museum has a whole series of artistically bound prayerbooks from the 17th century to the turn of the 20th century. These silver bindings represent great value. The oldest among them, with embossed Biblical scenes on both sides, was made in the 17th century, probably in Amsterdam (No. 143).

According to its hallmark, the repoussé, acanthus decorated silver binding with the Hebrew name of the owner under a crown was made in Hannover-Altstadt in Germany, in 1696. It is also very artistic (No. 144). The neo-baroque silver binding of Rabbi Lipót Lów's Bible was made in 1850 (No. 145), while the silver filigree binding of the Sephardi festival prayerbook with acanthus on brown velvet is dated 1844 (No. 147). It was a Hungarian craftsman, György Sodomka of Nyitra (active from 1836),[36] who made the Museum's prayer-book binding which is silver filigree work on brown velvet (No. 146) in the middle of the last century.

Ivory and enamel decorated bindings became fashionable during the second half of the last century. Each one is a miniature masterpiece of the art of bookbinding. Generally, they are wedding presents. Silver mountings and enamel decorations were put on leather binding with the initials of the owner in the middle of the composition. Sometimes a Jewish symbol (like the Tablets of the Law) was added.

During morning prayers, males put philacteries on their forehead and left arm. The holders of these, the Tefillin boxes, are usually made of leather. The Museum has a set of such boxes made of silver. They are two squares that fit into each other. They were made in Lemberg in 1806–1807 (No. 154). A similar silver box, but more richly decorated, also made in Lemberg, was shown at the Frankfurt Synagogue Exhibition.[37]

It used to be the custom in Jewish families to wear amulets (Mezuzah) to protect their owners from the evil eye, accidents and misfortune. Generally, they were made of silver, but often their execution was as elaborate as jewelry. They were little compartments into which pieces of parchment were placed with a magic text on them, or—as some that can also be found at the Jewish Museum in Budapest—little metal discs with engraved text. One of the magic words is 'Shaddai', the name of the Lord. The amulets were worn mainly by Jews who lived in countries around the Mediterranean and those in the Near East. However, they were worn in Hungary too. Specially beautiful amulets were made in Italy. An example is the Museum's embossed, cartouche-shaped hanging Shaddai amulet with a cluster of grapes, the symbol of fertility, at the base (No. 155). Mid-18th century replicas can be found in other museums such as in the Historisches Museum of Frankfurt and the Cluny Museum, in Paris.[38]

The amulet showing the Sacrifice of Isaac (No. 158) was also made in Italy (Rome) at the end of the 18th century. The Museum's late 18th-century piece that might have been made in Austria or Hungary has an arched top and two square twisted, crowned columns (No. 157) as well as the 19th-century amulet in the shape of a Torah Ark with two columns (No. 156), though similarly shaped pieces were also made in Italy. The 19th-century openwork, tendril-ornamented piece of the Museum is a good example of the cylindrical amulets that can be opened (No. 160). The silver filigree Shaddai amulet with a clasp made in the beginning of the 19th century is probably Hungarian work (No. 159).

Circumcision (Berit Milah) is commanded in the Book of Genesis (17:10). It is the covenant between God and a son of His People which is a festive ceremony that takes place when the male child is eight days old. Circumcision is done with a special ritual knife, the Mohel's knife. The ornate handle is usually made of quartz, agate, jasper, amber, ivory and, seldom, of silver.

Among the Museum's Mohel knives an artistically worked, mother-of-pearl handled knife with standing leaves is outstanding (No. 161). So is the silver filigree handled knife which is probably Hungarian (No. 162). Both are from the early 19th century.

Worthy of special mention among the articles of varied function is the lavishly etched mother-of-pearl box (No. 164) with the pictures of the Sanctuary, the Wailing Wall in Jerusalem, and the Tomb of Rachel. The ivory ball that can be opened to reveal the miniature sculptured scene of the finding of Moses (No. 165) was probably made in the 18th century.

The Sabbath is a Jewish holiday ordained by the Bible. It is the most important day of the week and starts on Friday at sundown with the lighting of the Sabbath lamps and candles which are the symbols of a Jewish home. Initially, oil lamps decorated with Jewish symbols were used for the purpose. With time, types of six, eight, and ten-pointed, star-shaped lamps developed. The earliest, 14th-century example of the star-shaped Sabbath lamp has six points in the shape of a Mogen David (Shield of David, usually called Star of David). The six-pointed oil lamp is usually hung on a long chain and under it is a kettle-like tray to catch the dripping oil. There is a toothed lever in the chain; the height of the lamp above the table can be regulated with it. Generally, these lamps are made of copper or bronze, but examples of silver also occur. In the 17th and 18th centuries in Alsace-Lorraine (Metz) and Germany, many varieties of these lamps developed. Starting with the 19th century, candles came into use and eclipsed the use of the Sabbath oil lamps. One of the Museum's Sabbath lamps has little decoration; it is a functional piece (No. 163).

Sanctification of the Sabbath starts with a blessing over a cup of wine, the Kiddush cup. This is followed by a festive meal in the light of the Sabbath lamp.

The 1845–1846 steel-engraved seat ticket, decorated with Biblical scenes, leads back into Hungarian Jewish history as it indicates the custom of purchasing seats in the synagogue by members of the congregation in Pest (No. 166). This synagogue, the Cultus Temple, stood at the site of today's Dohány utca Temple until the latter's dedication.

The metalwork collection of the Jewish Museum, made up of devotional pieces from synagogues and private homes is not only the largest group of objects in the Museum, but is also the most significant of any collection of its type in Europe.

NOTES

1. Sándor [Alexander] Scheiber: "Zsidó sarok az új régészeti kiállításon" [Jewish Corner in the New Archeological Exhibition], Új Élet XVIII (1962), No. 2, 2.
   Cf. Jewish Inscriptions in Hungary, Budapest–Leiden, 1983, 25–31.
2. Sándor Büchler: A zsidók története Budapesten a legrégibb időktől 1867-ig [Jewish History in Budapest from the Earliest Times to 1867], Budapest, 1901, 22–41.
3. Ibid.
4. Ibid.
5. Büchler: op. cit., 45–46.
6. László Zolnay: "Középkori zsinagógák a budai várban" [Synagogues of the Middle Ages in the Castle of Buda], Budapest Régiségei XXII (1971), 271–284.
7. Büchler: op. cit., 47.
8. Büchler: op. cit., 169.
9. Büchler: op. cit., 270–271.
10. Büchler: op. cit., 269.
11. Synagoga. Jüdische Altertümer, Handschriften und Kultgeräte. Historisches Museum, Frankfurt am Main. 1961, No. 218.
12. Ilona P. Brestyánszky: Pest-budai ötvösség [Silversmiths of Pest-Buda], Budapest, 1977, 348.
13. P. Brestyánszky: op. cit., 294.
14. P. Brestyánszky: op. cit., 244.
15. P. Brestyánszky: op. cit., 222.
16. P. Brestyánszky: op. cit., 172.
17. P. Brestyánszky: op. cit., 320.
18. P. Brestyánszky: op. cit., 344.
19. Budapest műemlékei II [Monuments in Budapest II], Budapest, 1962, 494.
20. Sándor [Alexander] Scheiber: Magyar Zsidó Oklevéltár XVI [Hungarian Jewish Archives]. Budapest, 1974, 157, 283; P. Brestyánszky: op. cit., 24.
21. Büchler: op. cit., 283.
22. Budapest műemlékei II, 494.; Elemér Kőszeghy: Magyarországi ötvösjegyek a középkortól 1867-ig [Hungarian Silversmith Hallmarks from the Middle Ages to 1867], Budapest, 1936, 63. According to a former Jewish Museum of Óbuda collection plate inscription, in 1799 Moshe Tzoref was among the officers of the Hevrah in Óbuda.
23. Synagoga, No. 209.
24. P. Brestyánszky: op. cit., 224, 226.
25. P. Brestyánszky: op. cit., 291.
26. P. Brestyánszky: op. cit., 168.
27. P. Brestyánszky: op. cit., 303.
28. M. G. Koolik: Towers of Spice. The Israel Museum, Jerusalem, 1982, 8.
29. Koolik: op. cit., 11.
30. P. Brestyánszky: op. cit., 290.
31. P. Brestyánszky: op. cit., 299, No. 279; Koolik: op. cit., No. 28.
32. Synagoga, No. 309.
33. Synagoga, No. 368.
34. Synagoga, No. 369.
35. Imre Katona: A magyar kerámia és porcelán [Hungarian Ceramics and Porcelain], Budapest, 1948, 235.
36. Kőszeghy: op. cit., 279.
37. Synagoga, No. 278.
38. V.A. Klagsbald: Jewish Treasures from Paris, Jerusalem, 1982, No. 163.

SELECTED BIBLIOGRAPHY

P. Brestyánszky, Ilona : *Ismerjük meg a kerámiát* [An Introduction to Ceramics], Budapest, 1966

P. Brestyánszky, Ilona : "Pest-budai gyűjtőperselyek a Zsidó Múzeumban" [Collection Boxes of Pest-Buda in the Jewish Museum], *MIOK Évkönyv*, Budapest, 1983–84, 57–72

Budapest Műemlékei [Historical Monuments in Budapest] II, Budapest, 1962

Büchler, Sándor : *A zsidók története Budapesten a legrégibb időktől 1867-ig* [The History of the Jews from Ancient Times to 1867], Budapest, 1901

Das Staatliche Jüdische Museum in Prag, Prague, 1966

Egyházi Gyűjtemények Kincsei [Treasures of Ecclesiastical Collections], Exhibition Catalog of the Museum of Applied Arts, Budapest, 1979

Grünvald, Fülöp—Naményi, Ernő : *Budapesti zsinagógák* [Synagogues of Budapest], Budapest, 1949

Grünvald, Fülöp—Scheiber, Sándor [Alexander] : *Adalékok a magyar zsidóság településtörténetéhez a XVIII. század első felében* [Contribution to the History of Hungarian Jewish Settlement in the First Half of the 18th Century], Budapest, 1963. Reprint from the Hungarian Jewish Archives, vol. VII

"Heilige Gemeinde Wien" Judentum in Wien. Sammlung Berger. Sonderausstellung 108. Historisches Museum der Stadt Wien. 1988

Katona, József : *A 90 éves Dohány utcai templom* [The 90-year-old Dohány Street Temple], Budapest, 1949

Katz, K.—Kahane, P. P.—Broschi, M. : *From the Beginning*. The Israel Museum, Jerusalem, 1968

Kaniel, M. : *Judaism*, Poole, Dorset, 1979

Kayser, S.—Schoenberger, A. : *Jewish Ceremonial Art*, Philadelphia, 1955

Koolik, M.G. : *Towers of Spice*, The Israel Museum, Jerusalem, 1982

Krüger, R. : *Die Kunst der Synagoge*, Leipzig, 1968

A régi Buda és Pest iparművészetének kiállítása [The Exhibition of Applied Art in Old Buda and Pest], Budapest, 1935

Narkiss, M. : *The Hanukkah Lamp*, Jerusalem, 1977

Scheiber, Alexander : *Hungarian Jewish Archives*, vol. XVI, Budapest, 1974

Scheiber, Sándor [Alexander] : *Folklór és tárgytörténet I–II* [Folklore and the History of Objects I–II], Budapest, 1977

Sachar, I. : *Jewish Tradition in Art*, Jerusalem, 1981

Stahl, A. : *The Torah Scroll*, The Israel Museum, Jerusalem, 1979

Synagoga. Jüdische Altertümer, Handschrift und Kultgeräte, Historisches Museum, Frankfurt am Main, 1961

Weinstein, Jay : *A Collectors' Guide to Judaica*, London, 1985

THE FOLLOWING BOOKS OF HALLMARKS WERE USED FOR THE IDENTIFICATION OF OBJECTS :

P. Brestyánszky, Ilona : *Ismerjük meg a kerámiát* [An Introduction to Ceramics], Budapest, 1966

P. Brestyánszky, Ilona : *Pest-budai ötvösség* [Silversmith of Pest-Buda], Budapest, 1977

Hintze, E. : *Süddeutsche Zinngiesser und ihre Marken*, Vol. 1–7, Leipzig, 1921–1931

Kőszeghy, Elemér : *Magyarországi ötvösjegyek a középkortól 1867-ig* [Hungarian Silversmith Hallmarks from the Middle Ages to 1867], Budapest, 1936

Reitzner, V. : *"Alt-Wien" Kunstlexikon*, Wien, 1952

Rosenberg, M. : *Der Goldschmiede Merkzeichen I–IV*, Frankfurt am Main, 1922–1928

Tardy : *Poinçons d'argent*, Paris, n.d.

1 Fleece Cup
Partially gilt silver, embossed and
engraved. Its cone-shaped body
widens upwards and has engraved
fleece decoration. There is a round
wreath under the rim with a stylized
crest in it that is a later engraving.
No marking

Hungarian
Early 17th century
Height: 11 cm.
Lip: 8 cm.
Base: 6.5 cm.
Inventory No.: 64.141

2 Beaker

Partially gilt silver, engraved and embossed. Cylindrical body. Six big flowers over the base. Its waist is a leaf-decorated lambrequin. In its side, engraved, in three round medallions heads of antique warriors in helmets. A garlanded and fruit-decorated lambrequin at the rim. Near the edge is the Hebrew inscription engraved later: "This cup belongs to the Holy Society of Óbuda, made in 509 [1749]". "The noble Gumpel, the noble Wolf and the noble Gerson"; "For an everlasting memorial to the Hevrah Kaddishah in Pest, from me, Mózes Holitscher, in the year of 638 [1878], as per the minor reckoning of years" (i. e., omitting the thousands).
"IM" mark on the rim
Hungarian
Early 17th century
Height: 28.5 cm.
Lip: 11.5 cm.
Base: 9.5 cm.
Inventory No.: 64.130
Exhibited: Treasures of Ecclesiastical Collections. No. 367

3 Long-stemmed Beaker

Partially gilt silver. Embossed. Leaf-decoration around the base. On the body, three masks in medallions among curved leaves and embossed flowers. Hebrew inscription on the widening lip: "It belongs to the local Hevrah Kaddishah of Pest".
"MN" mark
Hungarian
First half of the 17th century
Height: 15 cm.
Lip: 7 cm.
Base: 6.3 cm.
Inventory No.: 64.131
Exhibited: Treasures of Ecclesiastical Collections. No. 370

4 "Bunch of Grapes" Goblet

Partially gilt silver. Embossed with molded ornamentation. Stylized leaf design on the round base. There is a woodcutter child with bird on the stem which has the form of a sculptured tree-trunk. The bowl looks like a cluster of grapes with embossed bubbles. A silver-leafed rosette on the top and a molded bouquet of flowers. The engraved Hebrew inscription on the base: "As a gift of love to the Hevrah Kaddishah in Pest, Léb Pollák, in the year 596 according to the minor reckoning [1836]".

Nuremberg hallmark on the rim and Georg Müller's mark

Early 17th century

Height: 35 cm.

Lip: 9 cm.

Base: 7.7 cm.

Inventory No.: 64.132

Rosenberg III. No. 4192

Exhibited: The Hungarian Historical Silversmith Exhibition, Budapest, 1884, gallery 3, showcase 2, No. 25

5 Tankard

Gilt silver. Embossed. Curved leaf-wreath on the base. Two rows of high-embossed shell decoration on the cylindrical body with engraved Renaissance roses between them. There are six embossed shells on its arched top and the engraved Hebrew inscription: "This was donated to the Hevrah Kaddishah by Jakob Berlin. His memory be blessed, according to the minor reckoning, in 570 [1810]". In the center of the lid is the handle in the form of a molded brood-hen. The two sides of the hinge are angel heads and the handle has the form of a beaded question mark.
Nuremberg hallmark and Hanss Reif's mark
Mid-17th century

Height: 16.5 cm.
Lip: 10.8 cm.
Base: 12 cm.
Inventory No.: 64.129
Rosenberg III. No. 4134
Exhibited: Treasures of Ecclesiastical Collections. No. 372

6 Tankard

Silver, embossed, engraved. Upward tapering body. There are two embossed bunches of fruit on the side. The handle has rocaille decoration. The lid has a ball for a handle. Around, under the lip, is the engraved Hebrew inscription, "Behold, the old tankard bought by the officers in charge of charity of the Hevrah Kaddishah in Óbuda in the year of 552 [1792]". Augsburg hallmark on the rim and "MS" mark
17th century

Height: 21.5 cm.
Lip: 9.5 cm.
Base: 10.5 cm.
Inventory No.: 64.136
Rosenberg I. No. 529

7 Goblet

Gilt silver, embossed and engraved.
Leaf and curve decoration on the tall
and articulated stem and base. The
knop is vase shaped, with three arches.
The cup itself has lavishly chased
flower and fruit decoration in the
midst of which are three animal figures
with a landscape background. Later,
the Hebrew inscription had been engraved. "Brief Gedalyah's gift to the Hevrah Kaddishah in lieu of the price of his
grave in the year of 590 [1830]".
Faded Augsburg hallmark
17th century
Height : 35.5 cm.
Lip : 11.8 cm.
Base : 10.8 cm.
Inventory No. : 64.135

8 Tankard

Partially gilt silver, embossed. Acanthus leaf and thistle garland on the cylindrical body. Engraved Hebrew inscription: "According to the minor reckoning year of 597 [1837] this was given by the chief officers and their deputies to the Hevrah Menuhah Nehonah" (Society of Proper Rest—another name for the burial society). According to the inscription on the handle, it was "etched by Izsák Werber [Warber?]". On the rim of the cover, the Hebrew inscription: "Donated by the honorable Móse Bogdán in memory of his son Zehel".

Breslau hallmark on the rim and "HP" mark

Mid-17th century

Height: 14.7 cm.

Lip: 11.1 cm.

Base: 14.5 cm.

Inventory No.: 64.72

Rosenberg I. No. 1369, 1423

Exhibited: Treasures of Ecclesiastical Collections. No. 369

9 Tankard

Partially gilt silver. Embossed. Acanthus leaf decorated base. The body has high embossed rich leaf garland with two big flowers. In the middle of the lid is a handle that rises out of a flower. The handle is rocaille decorated. Under the lip is the engraved Hebrew inscription, "The property of the sick visiting society of Kanizsa. In the year of 569 (1809), according to the minor reckoning".

Salzburg hallmark and "HC" mark
18th century
Height : 15 cm.
Lip : 8.5 cm.
Base : 10.5 cm.
Inventory No. : 64.463
Reitzner 239

10 Beaker

Gilt silver, embossed, engraved, chased. Used to be the upper part of a stemmed cup. On the outward tapering cone body, in three oval medallions, are landscapes with deer, lion, and horse. Between the frames are embossed curved foliate designs with three herms with angels' wings. On the rim, near the lip, is the Hebrew engraved inscription, "A gift to the Hevrah Kaddishah in Pest according to the minor reckoning in 607 [1847], from me, Hayyim Spitzer".
No mark. German
First half of the 17th century
Height : 21.5 cm.
Lip : 10.5 cm.
Base : 7.5 cm.
Inventory No. : 64.133

10

11 Goblet

Silver, embossed, engraved. Leaf garland on its articulated base. The vase-shaped knop has three rocaille arches. The cup is decorated with curved stylized flowers. Under the rim the engraved Hebrew inscription, "Property of the Israelic congregation in Kanizsa. In the year of 563 [1803]".
No mark
German
17th century
Height : 26 cm.
Lip : 10.5 cm.
Base : 9.5 cm.
Inventory No. : 64.134

12 Cup with Cover

Silver, cast, embossed. On the downward tapering cone-shaped body are three birds in leaf garlands. There is a fruit cluster wreath on the articulated and arched cover. In the middle stands a molded antique warrior with lance and shield. On the rim, under the lip, the engraved Hebrew inscription, "This was donated by the orphans of Zalimer Teben to the Hevrah Kad-dishah in Pest, according to the minor reckoning in the year 570 [1810]".
Intertwined initials "CH" on the bottom
German
17th century
Height : 17 cm.
Lip : 9 cm.
Base : 7 cm.
Inventory No. : 64.128

13 Cup with Cover

Gilt silver, embossed, engraved. Stands on three balls for legs. At each leg, a white silver filigree work flower with richly stylized leaf decoration. At the top of the cylindrical body is the Hebrew engraved inscription, "Love offering to the holy society in Pest, the Hevrah Kaddishah, by Elhanan Yidels. According to the minor reckoning, in 579 [1819]". In the middle of the cover is a white silver filigree leaf rosetta and a ball for a handle.

Augsburg hallmark and Johann Wagner's mark
Early 18th century
Height: 15.5 cm.
Lip: 10.5 cm.
Base: 11 cm.
Inventory No.: 64.344. 1–2
Rosenberg I. No. 689

14 Goblet

Silver gilt, embossed, engraved. On it
bubbled base and cup are five each o
the scenes of the ten plagues of Egypt
in two rows. On top, under the lip is the
engraved Hebrew text from the Pass
over Haggadah, "These are those ter
plagues with which the Holy One—Hi
Name be blessed—punished the Egyp
tians".
Warsaw hallmark
18th century
Height : 20 cm.
Lip : 10.5 cm.
Base : 7 cm.
Inventory No. : 64.435
Rosenberg IV. No. 8119

15 Beaker
(Plate I)

Partially gilt silver, embossed, with base
On the body are niello scenes of the life
of Moses crossing the Red Sea, drawing
of the water, the two Tablets of the Law
etc. Engraved on the rim is the Hebrew
inscription, "Gift to the Hevrah Kad
dishah in Pest, according to the mino
reckoning, in 607 [1847]".
Moscow hallmark (1804) and "AB. HH
mark
Height : 17.5 cm.
Lip : 10.6 cm.
Base : 9.8 cm.
Inventory No. : 64.127
Tardy 353
Exhibited : Treasures of Ecclesiastica
Collections. No. 385

16 Cup with Base

Silver, embossed, engraved. An engraved upright leaf wreath on the round base. Three rocaille cartouches on the cone-shaped cup with a rose in the middle. Under the lip is engraved the Hungarian inscription, "As a sign of its respect, to Chief Rabbi Lipót Lőw of Nagykanizsa, the Israelite congregation of Pest in 1844".
Viennese hallmark (1844) and "AW" (Louis Vaugoin) on the body of the cup
Height: 22.5 cm.
Lip: 10 cm.
Base: 12 cm.
Inventory No.: 64.1108
Reitzner No. 1423

17

17 Goblet

Silver, embossed. Arched, articulated base, embossed stem, upward widening cup also ribbed and embossed, with the Hebrew engraved inscription in two fields: "The property of the Hevrah Kaddishah in Óbuda, 1874."
Buda hallmark (1851) and József Gretschl, Jr.'s mark
Height: 16.2 cm.
Lip: 9.5 cm.
Base: 7.7 cm.
Inventory No.: 64.68
Kőszeghy No. 354; *P. Brestyánszky* Nos. 33, 56

/ Beaker (Cat. No. 15)

II Pair of Rimmonim (Cat. No. 19)

III Torah Crown (Cat. No. 31)

IV Torah Breastplate (Cat. No. 38)

V Seder Plate (Cat. No. 118)

VI Seder Plate (Cat. No. 119)

VII/a Seder Plate (Cat. No. 126)

VII/b Seder Plate (Cat. No. 127)

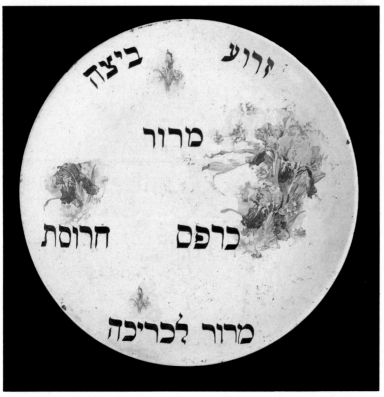

18 Goblet with Cover
(Elijah Cup)

Silver, embossed, engraved. The Prophet Isaiah, Noah and two persons tying wheat shown on the cup. The work of Margit Tevan (1901–1978).

1937
Height : 21 cm.
Lip : 9 cm.
Base : 8 cm.
Inventory No. : 64.163

19 Pair of Rimmonim
(Plate II)

Partially gilt silver, embossed and cast. An embossed branch with shells and leaves runs around the stem and the round base. The three-tiered crown is turret shaped. Three bells hang from the bottom, between them are six rounded flower garlands from three of which hangs a bunch of grapes and from the other three, a pomegranate. Above these are three little compartments in a vertical position. In the compartments are cast figures representing objects of the Sanctuary in Jerusalem. The objects in the second tier illustrate the clothes of the High Priest. On top of those compartments is an arch divided into six with shell and leaf decorations and six stylized leaves. This is topped by an embossed bunch of flowers in a vase. The Hebrew engraved inscription on the base, "Abraham Sopher, 561 (?) [1701] according to the minor reckoning".

Mark of Angielo Scarbello d'Este Padova (was used in Nagykanizsa)
Height : 70 cm.
Diameter : 10 cm.
Inventory No. : 64.378. 1–2
Rosenberg IV. No. 7421
Bibliography : F. Gambarin : La Magnifica Comunita di Este nella dialettica religiosa e civile. Padova, 1981
Analogue : B. C. Roth : *Jewish Art.* Tel-Aviv, 1961.
Illustration No. 142 ; A. Stahl : *The Torah Scroll.* 19

18

20 Rimmon (Finial)

Copper, embossed, engraved. There are two knops with engraved garlands on its stem. The top, in the form of a pomegranate, is decorated with engraved pomegranates. Engraved on the top rim is the inscription, "Tzvi Hersh, son of David, 362 [1602] according to the minor reckoning". On the lower edge is "The Sephardi [Spanish and Portuguese] congregation in Pest".
Turkish (?)
Late 16th century
Height: 34 cm.
Diameter: 8.5 cm.

Inventory No.: 64.386
Bibliography: A. Scheiber: *Jewish Inscriptions in Hungary*. 402–406.

21 Rimmon

Partially gilt silver, embossed. Round base. There is a ring on the cylindrical stem with erect leaf decoration. Its upper part is a four-arched crown. There is a bell inside the crown. Its engraved Hebrew inscription is, "Owned by the Holy Society here in Pest".
Viennese hallmark (1754) and "JB" monogram (Joseph Böheim)
From the Hevrah Kaddishah of Pest
Height: 19.5 cm.

Diameter: 5 cm.
Inventory No.: 64.10. 1–2
Reitzner No. 377

22 Pair of Rimmonim

Partially gilt silver, embossed, engraved. The tall stem and round base have engraved flower garlands on them. The body itself is lavishly embossed with stylized leaf and flower decoration over which is an acanthus leaf frieze. On top is a four-arched open crown. On the crown is the double tablet of the Ten Commandments with the opening words.

Viennese hallmark, the trademark of Ignatius Packeny (Pageni, mentioned 1807–1821) and Viennese tax stamp
From the Holy Society of Nagykanizsa
Height: 30 cm.
Diameter: 7.8 cm.
Inventory No.: 64.377. 1–2
Reitzner No. 1132

23 Pair of Rimmonim

Gilt silver, embossed, engraved. A row of pearls on its round base. It stem is flower patterned. The knop has two wreaths of erect leaves. On top is an eight-arched open crown with a bell inside. Over that is a double-headed molded eagle.

Viennese hallmark on its base (1797 and faded "I. J." mark
From the Holy Society of Óbuda
Height: 37 cm.
Diameter: 9.5 cm.
Inventory No.: 64.51 1–2

22

24 Pair of Rimmonim

Gilt silver, embossed, engraved. On the round profiled base is a row of erect leaves. In the middle of the cylindrical stem is a belt of tulips, erect leaves and palmetto designs. The top is a crown of twelve arches with bells. The top of the crown is shaped like a fir-cone.

Viennese hallmark (1807) and "CCL" (Christoph Lehman?) mark

From the Holy Society of Nagykanizsa

Height: 34 cm.

Diameter: 12 cm.

Inventory No.: 64.410. 1–2

Reitzner No. 1141

25 Pair of Rimmonim

Silver, embossed, engraved, with a round base. Its stem is shaped like a column with milled rings. The top has rosette leaf decoration and three bells. The gilt silver crown is divided into four parts ornamented with engraved leaf garlands. On top is a crowned double-headed eagle.

Viennese hallmark (1810) and "I. F." (Joseph Feyerabendt) mark

From the Hevrah Kaddishah of Pest

Height: 34 cm.

Diameter: 12.5 cm.

Inventory No.: 64.8. 1–2

Reitzner No. 880

26 Pair of Rimmonim

Silver, embossed, engraved. The round base has a milled ring. The stem is column-shaped with leaf and rosette decoration on top, and three bells. The divided open crown is decorated with embossed leaves. Inside there is a bell.

On top is a crowned double-headed molded eagle.

Hallmark of in Pozsonyvártelek (1810) and Frigyes Becker, Sr's mark

Height : 27.5 cm.

Diameter : 10 cm.

Inventory No. : 64.391. 1–2

Kőszeghy Nos. 1810, 1853

27 Pair of Rimmonim

Partially gilt silver. Around its round base is the engraved Hebrew inscription, "To the new synagogue in Miskolc according to the minor reckoning, in the year of 623 [1863]". On the base are leaf and flower decorations. The cylindrical stem is engraved to imitate the trunk of a palmtree. The upper part is a row of hanging leaves with eight bells. The top is bell-like with a row of hanging leaves and a round knop.

Viennese hallmark (1818) and "KI" mark

From the Holy Society of Pest

Height : 33 cm.

Diameter : 10.5 cm.

Inventory No. : 64.29. 1–2

26

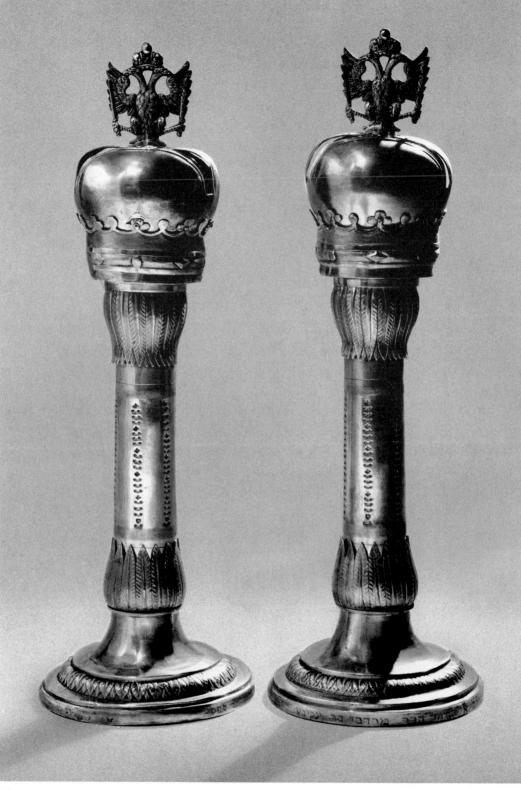

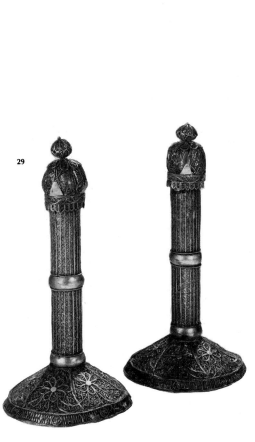

29

28 Pair of Rimmonim
Partially gilt silver, embossed, engraved. Wreath on the round base and engraved Hebrew inscription. Small flower garlands and a collar of leaves on the cylindrical stem. There is a big crown on top the hoop with gemlike decoration. Inside are bells. On top is a crowned double-headed eagle. The inscription reads, "Graciously donated to the Holy Society in Óbuda by Mordecai Blau, son of Akiba of blessed memory, and his spouse, Frádl, daughter of Mendel, in the year 600 [1840] according to the minor reckoning".
Pest hallmark (around 1800) and Ferenc Pasperger's mark

Height : 43 cm.
Diameter : 14.5 cm.
Inventory No. : 64.67. 1–2
Kőszeghy Nos. 487, 393 ; *P. Brestyánsz-ky* Nos. 118, 200, 284
Exhibited : Exhibition of Industrial Art in Old Buda and Pest. No. 32

29 Pair of Rimmonim
Partially gilt silver with filigree decoration. Abundant filigree work on the convex base and cylindrical stem. At the top is a small crown topped by a ball. The crown is decorated with filigree leaves and has a bell inside.
No mark
Óbuda (?)
From the Hevrah Kaddishah of Óbuda

Late 18th century
Height : 27 cm.
Diameter : 11.5 cm.
Inventory No. : 64.70. 1–2

30 Rimmon
Ivory and wood. Turned and carved. Contoured base and twisted stem on which is an ivory hand holding a rounded cylinder that ends in a ball-shaped point. The Hebrew inscription is burnt into it : "Gift of the members of the Mishna Society, Krivoi Rog".
Russia
Late 18th century, early 19th century
Height : 25 cm.
Radius : 15 cm.
Inventory No. : 66.43

31 Torah Crown (Keter)
(Plate III)
Partially gilt silver, cast, embossed. Six prancing lions hold up the upper, smaller, crown. The upper part has white silver erect leaf decoration and fir-cone. The lower part has six red glass beads.
Cracow
Cracow duty stamp (1806–1807) on the top
Mid-18th century
Height : 21 cm.
Diameter : 11 cm.
Inventory No. : 64.413
Reitzner No. 204
Analogue : A. Stahl : *The Torah Scroll*. Illustration No. 20

32 Torah Crown
Gilt silver, embossed, with shell and leaf decoration. It is a closed type crown with six bands. On top is a bell attached and has the inscription, "Belongs to the Hevrah Kaddishah here in Pest". The top is a fir-cone.

Viennese hallmark (1754) and "IB" (Joseph Böheim) monogram
Height : 20.5 cm.
Diameter : 15 cm.
Inventory No. : 64.12
Reitzner No. 1377

33 Torah Crown
Partially gilt silver, embossed. The hoop has a row of beads and Hebrew inscription. Over the hoop is a stylized acanthus-leaf headdress. It is a closed crown type with six bands. The bands have interwoven decoration with stylized flowers and colored glass beads. The Hebrew inscription : "To the congregation in Kanizsa, in the year 556 [1796] according to the minor reckoning".
Vienna
Viennese customs stamp (1809–1810)
Second half of the 18th century
Height : 33 cm.
Diameter : 22 cm.
Inventory No. : 64.370
Reitzner No. 205

34 Torah Crown
Partially gilt silver, embossed, chased. Coronet type. The oval base is combined with two finials. Each of the Rimmonim has 13 bells on mullion work and a closed crown topped by a double-headed eagle. There is a palmette row on the hoop under which is the Hebrew inscription : "To the Holy Society in Óbuda, in the year of 566 [1806] to the minor reckoning". Pest hallmark (G year-letter, 1774–1781) and János Mihály Schwager's mark
Height : 43.5 cm.
Diameter : 30 cm.
Inventory No. : 64.45
Kőszeghy Nos. 482, 389, 452 ; P. Brestyánszky Nos. 114, 316, 194
Exhibited : Exhibition of Applied Art in Old Buda and Pest. No. 28 ; Treasures of Ecclesiastical Collections. No. 378

35 Torah Crown
Gilt silver, embossed, engraved. Coronet type combined with two Rimmonim. On the hoop, between two rows of beads is an engraved leaf garland. Above the rows of beads, rocailles and acanthus leaves. The cylindrical finials end in a fir-cone each and around them, on engraved twisted stem are mullions with bells. Above each is a closed crown with double-headed eagle.
Pest hallmark (1793–1797) and János Müller's mark
Height: 43 cm.
Diameter: 30 cm.

Inventory No.: 64.46
Kőszeghy Nos. 396, 457, 485; *P. Brestyánszky* Nos. 274, 99, 116
Exhibited: Exhibition of Applied Art in Old Buda and Pest. No. 29

36 Torah Breastplate
Gilt silver, embossed in the shape of an Ark of the Torah with shell decoration on a punched ground. On the two sides, two rampant lions stand on twisted columns and in the middle is a calendar tablet frame. On top is a leaf-decorated coronet with the Hebrew inscription: "The Holy Society here in Pest".
Viennese hallmark [1754] and "IB" (Joseph Böheim) monogram
Height: 21 cm.
Width: 15 cm.
Inventory No.: 64.5
Reitzner No. 1377

Exhibited: Treasures of Ecclesiastical Collections. No. 375

37 Torah Breastplate
Partially gilt silver, embossed, engraved. It has a small shelled and latticed cartouche with the engraved Hebrew inscription, "The work was finished in the year 539 [1779] according to the minor reckoning", in the middle. In the center there is a little compartment with an acanthus leaf crown for the Ten Commandments. On the two sides are roses with bunches of grapes. On each side of the crown is a shield-shaped cartouche above two columns, the outer ones with a prancing lion on top. The canopy on top has a double-headed heraldic eagle.
Pest hallmark (1779) and János Mihály Schwager's mark
Height : 47.7 cm.
Width : 28 cm.
Inventory No. : 64.52

Kőszeghy Nos. 482, 389, 452 ; P. Brestyánszky Nos. 114, 194, 316
Exhibited : Exhibition of Applied Art in Old Buda and Pest. No. 28

38. Torah Breastplate
(Plate IV)
Partially gilt silver filigree on silver base in the shape of an arched Ark of the Torah. At the bottom is a cartouche-shaped frame holding the discs designating a holiday. It also has a long chain on which it is suspended from the Torah. In the middle of the breastplate between two columns is an ogival double door, an inscription with date and a turquoise decorated rosette. Behind the doors are the two tablets of the Ten Commandments and their initial words. On top is a crown.
No mark
Balkans (?), (Turkish ?)

Late 17th century (?)
Height : 14 cm.
Width : 12 cm.
Inventory No. 64.399

39 Torah Breastplate
Silver, embossed, in the shape of an Ark of the Torah with relief figures of Moses and Aaron on the two sides. Canopy on top and the two tablets with the Ten Commandments under it. Engraved : "Pesther isr. Gemeinde" (Israelite congregation of Pest). Closed crown on top.
Viennese hallmark (1805) and "FLT" (Franz Lorenz Turinsky) mark
Height : 14.5 cm.
Width : 12 cm.
Inventory No. : 64.27
Reitzner No. 947

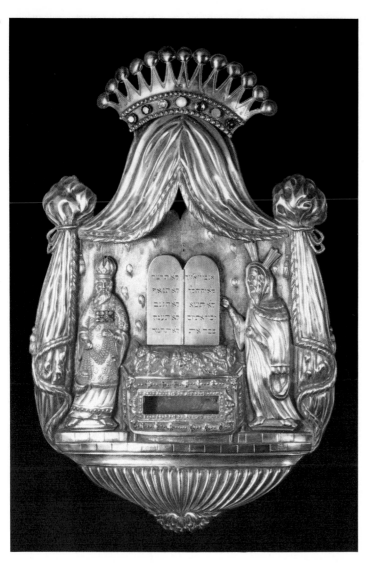

40 Torah Breastplate
Partially gilt silver, embossed. Shield-shape cartouche with balcony and the figures of Moses and Aaron, one on each side, and the two tablets of the Ten Commandments with the Hebrew initial words in the middle. Under this, with angel heads and flowers decorated a calendar tablet frame. The top is a thirteen-pointed bejeweled coronet.
Viennese tax stamp (1807)
Height: 49 cm.

Width: 30 cm.
Inventory No.: 64.734
Reitzner No. 204

41 Torah Breastplate
Partially gilt, silver, embossed, punched, with a calendar tablet frame and the engraved inscription, "To the Holy Society in Óbuda, according to the minor reckoning, in 600 [1840]". Its bell-shaped upper part is leaf and rose-garland decorated. There is a canopy on each side and double col-

umns with a prancing lion on top holding a shield. Between the two pairs of lions are the two tablets of the Ten Commandments with the initial words. Above them is a crown. A molded, crowned, double-headed eagle is on top.
Viennese hallmark (1807) and "FL" (Friedrich Laubenbacher, Jr.) mark
Height: 50 cm.
Width: 32.5 cm.
Inventory No.: 64.53
Reitzner No. 1157

42 Torah Breastplate

Partially gilt silver, embossed, chased. Cartouche shaped. There are embossed roses with stylized acanthus leaves at the bottom. A shell-decorated calendar tablet frame is in the middle. Above it, double doors in the shape of the two tablets of the Ten Commandments with engraved Hebrew inscription. Left and right, a rampant lion. Acanthus-leaf decorated big crown on top. Below is the engraved Hebrew inscription, "In memory of Izsák and Rozália Grósz, their daughter, Mrs. Mózes Ehrlich".

Viennese hallmark (1850) and "CSS" (Christ, Sender) monogram
Height: 53 cm.
Width: 36 cm.
Inventory No.: 64.2
Reitzner No. 1325/a

43 Torah Breastplate

Silver, punched, chased. The calendar tablet frame is towards the bottom, with rose decoration under it. In the cartouche field, framed in flaming rocailles, a lion stands on each side on a column holding the Torah Crown over the two tablets of the Ten Commandments with the first words of the Decalogue.
Pest hallmark (1864) and Pál Cseh's mark
Height : 25 cm.
Width : 24 cm.
Inventory No. : 64.74
Kőszeghy No. 559; *P. Brestyánszky* Nos. 172, 240

44 Torah Breastplate

Silver, embossed. Cartouche-shaped with baldachine. Shell and stylized leaf decoration in relief at the bottom. On the two sides, on a punched background, double-tailed crowned lions stand on columns and hold a Torah crown over the two tablets of the Ten Commandments on which the initial words of the Decalogue are engraved. Under the tablets is the calendar tablet frame.
Viennese hallmark (1861) and "JD" (Joseph Dangl) trademark
Height : 36 cm.
Width : 27 cm.
Inventory No. : 64.401
Reitzner No. 1426

43

44

45

45 Torah Pointer (Yad)
Silver, embossed, with a square and
twisted stem. There is a ball in the
middle and at the end, with a chain.
The other end is a hand with a point-
ing right index finger.
Prague hallmark and "TH" monogram
(1814–1866)
Early 19th century
From the property of the Hevrah Kad-
dishah in Pest
Height : 27 cm.
Inventory No.: 64.13
Rosenberg III. No. 5001

46 Torah Pointer
Silver, embossed. Its triangular stem
is divided into squares. There is a flat
cube on a half-sphere at the two ends
and the middle. At one end is a chain,
a pointing right hand at the other. A

Hebrew inscription on the wide rim,
"Mose Reich, R. Yaacov Rodwan,
Mose Rotter, Benjamin Schafe, R.
Enzl, Itzik Laib, in the 599 year [1839]
according to the minor reckoning,
the officers of the Hevrah Kaddishah
in the city of Óbuda".
Buda hallmark (1834) and József Ká-
roly Gretschl, Sr's mark
Height : 28 cm.
Inventory No.: 64.80
Kőszeghy No. 354; *P. Brestyánszky*
Nos. 26, 56
Exhibited : Exhibition of the Industrial
Art in Old Buda and Pest. No. 49

47 Torah Pointer
Silver, embossed. Cylindrical and
fluted stem divided by three balls.
There is a pointing hand at one end.
Viennese hallmark (1858) and "JD"

(Joseph Dangl) monogram
Height : 27 cm.
Inventory No.: 64.30
Reitzner No. 1426

48 Torah Pointer
Silver, chased, with three flat cubes
on its square stem which has etched
decoration. A chain at one end, a
pointing right hand at the other. En-
graved Hebrew inscription: "1837".
Óbuda hallmark (1836) and Fülöp
Adler's mark
Height : 29 cm.
Inventory No.: 64.81
Kőszeghy No. 375; *P. Brestyánszky*
No. 97
Exhibited : Exhibition of Applied Art in
Old Buda and Pest. No. 37

86

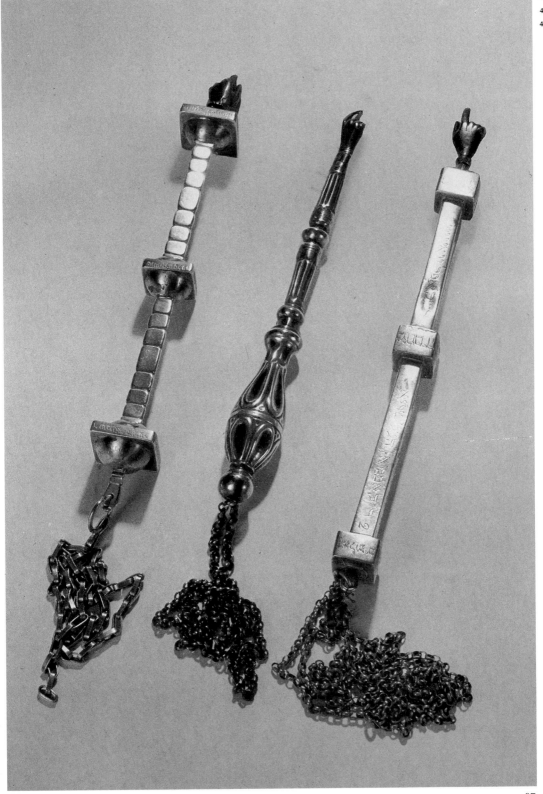

49 Torah Pointer
Wood, carved, with movable round
ring links and ball at one end and a
pointing right hand at the other.
No mark
Transylvanian
Mid to late 19th century, early 20th
century
Height: 40 cm.
Inventory No.: 66.48

49

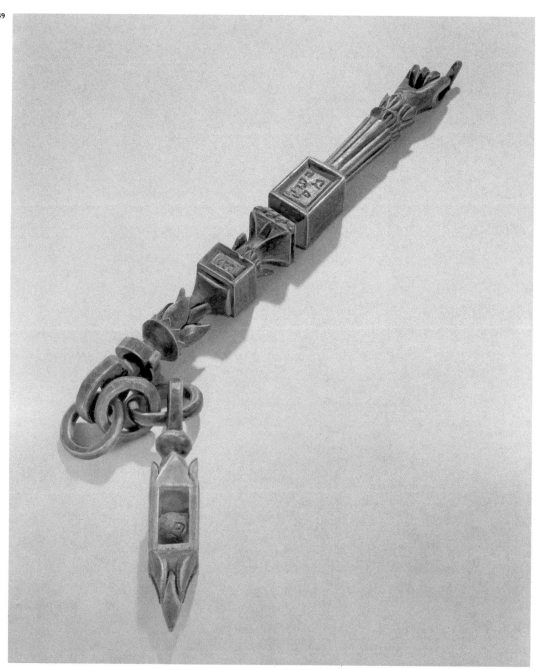

50 Mug for Washing Hands
Tinned brass, embossed. Cone shaped, with two big handles.
No mark
Hungarian (?)
18th century
Height: 13.5 cm.
Lip: 11 cm.
Inventory No.: 64.352

51 Cohen's Laver
Tinned brass, chased. High, contoured rim with four bands. Engraved Hebrew inscription on the underside of the rim, "The gift of Sámuel, the Levite, from his congregation in Nikolsburg, in the year 594 [1834] according to the minor reckoning".
No mark
Hungarian
Mid-18th century
Height: 40 cm.
Width: 28.5 cm.
Inventory No.: 64.355

52 Cohen's Pitcher
Pewter, cast, with round contoured base, pear-shaped body, wide mouth and rocaille handle.
No mark
Hungarian
Mid-18th century
Height: 19 cm.
Base: 9 cm.
Inventory No.: 64.356

53 Levi's Pitcher

Silver, oval, chased, engraved. High articulated base, the upper part ribbed and pear-shaped, with an extended spout and rocaille handle. On the body is the engraved Hebrew inscription, "This was donated by Salamon Rosenthal to the local Hevrah Kaddishah, Pest".
Viennese hallmark (1757) and "F. L." (Frantz Lintzberger) mark on the rim
Height: 18.5 cm.
Lip: 10.2 cm.
Inventory No.: 64.15
Reitzner No. 768
Exhibited: Treasures of Ecclesiastical Collections. No. 377

54 Levi's Bowl

Silver, chased, embossed, moulded, biscuit-shaped body. Engraved Hebrew inscription on the rim, "This was given as a memorial by the learned Salamon Rosenthal and his wife Hayele. May their souls be attached to the living. In 605 [1845] according to the minor reckoning. Hevrah Kaddishah, Pest".
"PD" monogram
Viennese
1757
Height: 3.5 cm.
Diameter: 37 cm.
Inventory No.: 64.16

55 Levi's Pitcher

Silver, embossed. Oval contoured base with tiny leaf-garland decoration. The pear-shaped body has a row of embossed erect leaves. The shoulder is decorated with a flower and leaf garland, and a row of beads. There is a stylized leaf garland on the neck. The pitcher has a wide beaded spout and a handle in the shape of a serpent.
Pest hallmark (1797) and József Prandtner's mark
Height: 40 cm.
Base: 10.5 cm.
Inventory No.: 64.47
Kőszeghy Nos. 491, 393, 458; *P. Brestyánszky* Nos. 119, 200, 296
Exhibited: Exhibition of Applied Art in Old Buda and Pest. No. 30; Treasures of Ecclesiastical Collections. No. 374

53
54

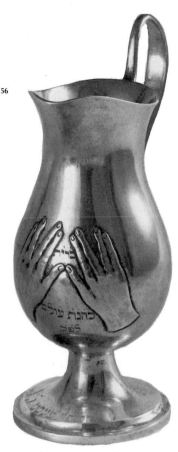

56 Cohen's Pitcher

Silver, embossed, round base, pear-shaped body. In front, in the middle in relief is the priestly symbol of two raised hands in blessing and also the engraved inscription, "Property of the Hevrah Kaddishah here in Pest". On the base: "For eternal priestly covenant in the year of 587 [1827] according to the minor reckoning". Wide spout and high ribbon-shaped handle.

Pest hallmark (1824) and Ferenc Schmidt's mark on the bottom

Height: 22.3 cm.

Diam. of base: 9 cm.

Inventory No.: 64.351

Kőszeghy Nos. 522, 400; *P. Brestyánszky* Nos. 130, 312

Exhibited: Exhibition of Applied Art in Old Buda and Pest. No. 39

57 Charity Bowl

Silver, chased, engraved, semispherical body with narrow rim and palmette handle. On the rim is the engraved inscription, "For the Hevrah Kaddishah in Óbuda, according to minor reckoning, the year 562 [1802]".

Pest hallmark, the letter "N" (for the year 1802) and Antal Müller's trademark on the rim

Diameter: 13.2 cm.

Inventory No.: 64.487

Kőszeghy Nos. 496, 459, 393; *P. Brestyánszky* Nos. 116, 272, 201

58 Charity Bowl

Silver, chased, engraved, semispherical body with horizontal rim and palmette handle. On the rim is the engraved inscription in Hebrew, "Made from the charity money of Itzig Totis's house of prayer, Hayim Spitz and Pesah Wachsbaum Gabbaim [officers], in Óbuda in the year of 581 [1821] according to the minor reckoning".

Buda hallmark (1815) and Pál Czigler's mark on the rim

Diameter: 12.7 cm.

Inventory No.: 64.486

Kőszeghy Nos. 343, 311; *P. Brestyánszky* Nos. 54, 18

Exhibited: Exhibition of Applied Art in Old Buda and Pest. No. 35

59 Funeral Charity Box
Silver, chased, engraved. Shaped like a grave. On top and in front are engraved scenes of the sick-bed, the bier, the washing of the dead and the funeral procession. Engraved is the Hebrew inscription, "The officers of the Holy Society of Pest ordered it to be made for the Hevrah Kaddishah, according to the minor reckoning, in the year 563 [1803]". Has a large stirrup handle.

Pest hallmark (1803) and Tamás Trautzl's mark
Height : 13.5 cm.
Inventory No. : 64.485
Kőszeghy Nos. 393, 501 ; *P. Brestyánszky* Nos. 119. 334
Exhibited : Exhibition of Industrial Art in Old Buda and Pest. No. 33. Treasures of Ecclesiastical Collections. No. 381

60

61

60 Charity Box

Silver, embossed, engraved. On the side of the cylindrical body is a shield decorated with a bunched ribbon and leaves. Molded snake handle and molded lion on top. There are engraved inscriptions on the side and shield: "This charity box was commissioned by the leading chief curators here at the Hevrah Kaddishah in Óbuda in memory of the dead. In the year 583 [1823] according to the minor reckoning".

Pest hallmark (1822) and Ferenc Pasperger's mark

94

Height: 19 cm.
Diameter: 8.7 cm.
Inventory No.: 64.513
Kőszeghy Nos. 487, 393, 458; *P. Brestyánszky* Nos. 284, 128
Exhibited: Exhibition of Applied Art in Old Buda and Pest. No. 38

61 Charity Plate with Base

Silver, embossed, engraved, with palmette design on its round base. The semispherical tray is divided into three parts and has a molded bunch of grapes in the middle. On the rim of the plate is the engraved Hebrew

inscription, "Donated to the Hevrah Kaddishah by the men here named in the year 602 [1842] according to the minor reckoning", followed by list of names.

Buda hallmark (1841) and József Károly Gretschl, Sr's. mark
Height: 15 cm.
Diameter: 15.5 cm.
Inventory No.: 64.478
Kőszeghy No. 354; *P. Brestyánszky* Nos. 56, 29
Exhibited: Exhibition of Industrial Art in Old Buda and Pest. No. 46

62 Covered Charity Box

Silver, embossed, engraved. The body stands on an oblong base with an angled handle on one side. There is a square opening on the embossed cover. The engraved Hebrew inscription in the rocaille-decorated cartouche in front, "Charity box of the congregation of Kanizsa. According to the minor reckoning 602 [1842]". Viennese hallmark (1840) and Louis Vaugoin or Alois Wackenroder mark Height: 20 cm.
Inventory No.: 64.507
Reitzner Nos. 1423, 1424

63 Covered Charity Box

Silver, embossed, engraved. The cylindrical body stands on an oval base. The latter and the bottom of the cover are decorated with a row of beads. The high embossed cover has a square opening. The handle is in the form of a question mark. Engraved Hebrew inscription in the front, "This alms box was paid for by the treasury of the Hevrah Kaddishah for use at funerals the ... chief curators ... curators here in Pest in 615 [1855] according to the minor reckoning". The German engraved inscription reads, "Verfertigt im Jahre 1855".

Pest hallmark (1855) and Ferenc Schmidt's mark
Height : 18 cm.
Diameter : 13 cm.
Inventory No. : 64.509
Kőszeghy Nos. 523, 163 ; *P. Brestyánszky* No. 312

64 Covered Charity Box

Partially gilt silver, embossed, engraved. The body has the form of a pitcher and cartouches lavishly decorated with tongues of flame, rocailles and roses. There is an embossed foliate band on the cover. The cover has a square opening. Engraved Hebrew

inscription on the front, "Society for the support of the poor and the unfortunate. Nagykanizsa. Made in the year 608 [1848] according to the minor reckoning".
Viennese hallmark (1848) and T. Mayerhoffer's mark
Height : 17 cm.
Diameter : 8 cm.
Inventory No. : 64.500
Reitzner No. 1307

65 Charity Box

Silver, embossed. Oblong body on oblong base. An Eternal Light in front, between two twisted columns. A small vase with flowers on the two narrower sides. The opening is on the embossed top. Its Hebrew inscription: "This almsbox belongs to the Eternal Society of the congregation in Kanizsa. Paid for from donations of good souls and finished in the year 614 [1854] according to the minor reckoning". Viennese hallmark (184[?]3) and Corn Sagg von Sach's mark
Height: 19 cm.
Length: 10 cm.
Inventory No.: 64.498
Reitzner No. 1294

66

66 Charity Box
Silver, chased. Cylindrical body, wide, thick questionmark-shaped handle. The Hebrew inscription on the body reads, "This charity box belongs to the Hevrah of the congregation in Óbuda. It was made at the order of the chief and deputy Gabbaim and supervisors in 624 [1864] according to the minor reckoning".
Pest hallmark (1864) and Ignác

Cserekviczky's mark
Height: 12.5 cm.
Diameter: 8.5 cm.
Inventory No.: 64.495
Kőszeghy No. 560; P. *Brestyánszky* Nos. 241, 172

67 Charity Bowl
Silver, chased. Flattened semispherical body. Has a small rim with engraved Hebrew inscription and year (1860).

67
68

Small handle.
On the back, inscribed, "Pest, isr. Gemeinde"
Pest hallmark (1859) and Pál Cseh's mark
Height : 8 cm.
Diameter : 20 cm.
Inventory No. : 64.484
Kőszeghy Nos. 559, 431 ; P. Brestyánszky Nos. 167, 240

68 Funeral Charity Box for the Poor
Silver, chased, engraved. On the front of the oval cylindrical body with oval base is the Hebrew inscription in an engraved wreath, "Donation by Ábrahám Weiss to the Hevrah Kaddishah according to the minor reckoning in 619 [1859]". On top of the arched, embossed cover is a square opening. The handle is in the shape of a question mark.
Pest hallmark (1858) and Pál Cseh's mark
Height : 18 cm.
Inventory No. : 64.496
Kőszeghy Nos. 559, 430 ; P. Brestyánszky Nos. 240, 166
Exhibited : Exhibition of Applied Art in Old Buda and Pest. No. 48 ; Treasures of Ecclesiastical Collections. No. 391

69 Spicebox
Silver, embossed, engraved. Round base and funnel-shaped stem with sharkskin twisted stripes. Above the stem is the turret-shaped compartment with clock face and openwork leaves on the side. There is a door in front that can be opened. On top are one large and four small turrets with openwork leaves. Each is topped by a ball and flag.
"l" hallmark of Nuremberg
Late 17th century
Height : 23.5 cm.
Inventory No : 64.172

70 Spicebox

Silver filigree. Six-sided base, six-lobed turret with three-tiered and balconied upper part. There is a movable little door in front. The center tier has a little bell inside and double window opening. The upper tier has little paired windows. A ball and flag at top.
Undecipherable mark

Eastern Europe
Late 18th century
Height: 27 cm.
Inventory No.: 64.174

71 Spicebox

Gilt silver, cast. Embossed wreath on the contoured round base. The stem is a molded tree branch with an erect lion under it. Higher up, five fruits. The top

is shaped like a pear. The two headed Polish eagles on the upper part among flower garlands on a chased base. The lid with a gilt bird on top can be lifted
Number 12 hallmark
Polish (Cracow)
Around 1830
Height: 19 cm.
Inventory No.: 64.203
Tardy No. 750

70
71
72

100

2 Spicebox

Silver filigree. The filigree square base stands on four palmette legs. The turret-shaped compartment has a balcony round it at the base, above which is a movable little door. On top of the turret is a ball and flag with the trade-mark "J. G.". Inside is a bell.
József Gretschl, Jr.'s mark
Buda
First half of the 19th century
Height: 33 cm.
Inventory No.: 64.171
Kőszeghy No. 354; P. Brestyánszky No. 56

73 Spicebox

Silver filigree. It stands on four legs that look like human feet. It has two tiers and has the shape of a turret. The first tier has a movable door and balcony. The second tier has a bell inside, a double window on each side, and a small flag on each corner. The top is a four-lobed ball with flag.
No mark
Óbuda (?)
Late 18th century
Height: 32 cm.
Inventory No.: 64.71

73

74 Spicebox
Silver filigree. Four-lobed base. The middle part is shaped like a turret, has a balcony around it and movable door in front. The upper part is dome-shaped with gilt flags.
No mark
Eastern Europe
Around 1830
Height: 18 cm.
Inventory No: 64.209

75 Spicebox
Silver, chased. The upward slanting cylindrical stem on a square base has an erect-leaf collar and the cylindrical upper part is checkered.
No mark

Late 18th century
Height: 14.5 cm.
Inventory No.: 64.189

76 Spicebox
Silver, embossed. The round base has a leaf wreath on it. The stem is short and cylindrical. The turret-shape upper part is brick engraved with an openwork balcony. Movable door in front, engraved double windows and rosettes on the sides. The two balconies have a ball and flag on each corner. Ball and flag on top.
"GG" trademark
Nuremberg
Late 18th century, early 19th century
Height: 18 cm.

Inventory No: 64.195
Rosenberg III. No. 3767

74
75
76

77 Spicebox

Silver filigree. Square base, filigree balustered knop, to the two-tiered balconied turret. On each of the four peaks of the first tier is a flag. The top has a balustered ball with a flag divided into two.

Pest hallmark and "WM" (Vince Messerschmied?, Wilhelm Meitinsky?) mark 1806–1810

Height: 25 cm.

Diameter: 6.8 cm.

Inventory No.: 64.193

P. Brestyánszky 290

78

79

81 Spicebox
Partially gilt silver, embossed, filigree. The tall square base stands on lion's paws. Four-sided shaft, two tiered turret body. The first story has a filigree balcony around it, a movable door and little flags on its points. On the arched top is a ball with flag on which is an engraved Hebrew inscription. On the sides are cameos of female heads and red and blue stones. The Hebrew inscription on the little flag reads, "Prepared from donations in the year 591 [1831] according to the minor reckoning". At the bottom is engraved, "Property of the Charity Society of Kanizsa".
Hungarian
1831
Height: 32 cm.
Diameter: 9.7 cm.
Inventory No.: 64.187

82 Spicebox
Silver filigree. Tall and wide contoured base that stands on four balls and a smooth rim. The body has the shape of a three-story turret. There is a balcony at the first tier, gilt silver flags on the corners of the second and third tiers. A movable door on the first floor and a bell inside. Pest hallmark (around 1860, the last digit of the number of the year is faded) and Ignác Cserekviczky's mark
Height: 33 cm.
Diameter of base: 9.5 cm.
Inventory No.: 64.169
Kőszeghy No. 560; P. Brestyánszky No. 241

78 Spicebox
Silver filigree. The eight-lobed base has four small and four large rosettes. The body is shaped like an orb, with the upper section removable. Leaves on top with a tiny ball.
No mark
Poland (?)
Early 19th century
Height: 19 cm.
Diameter: 8.5 cm.
Inventory No.: 64.186

79 Spicebox
Partially gilt silver, running filigree. Oblong base on four rounded legs. Four arched filigree surmounts. The rounded knop is ball-shaped. The turret is square filigree work with filigree spire topped by a flag. The turret has a door in front.
13 hallmark
Hungarian

First half of the 19th century
Height: 17 cm.
Diameter of base: 6 cm.
Inventory No.: 64.201
Analogue: M. G. Koolik: *Towers of Spice*. Illustration No. 34

80 Spicebox
Partially gilt silver, filigree. It is in the shape of a three-story turret. It has a tall filigree square base and knop. The first two tiers have a balcony and the first one has a movable door. The second and third have open windows. On top is a deer-shaped flag and a figure blowing a Shofar.
Viennese tax stamp (1810–1824) 19th century
Height: 37 cm.
Diameter of base: 6 cm.
Inventory No.: 64.168
Analogue: M. G. Koolik: *Towers of Spice*. Illustration No. 46

על הפסוק מזרועות ... בשנת תרל"א

83 Spicebox
Silver, cast, in the shape of a dove
with engraved feathers.
No mark
Hungarian, Viennese (?)
Late 19th century
Length : 7 cm.
Inventory No.: 64.226

84 Spicebox
Silver, cast, engraved, in the shape of
a fish. The movable body has thirteen
parts with engraved decoration. The
eyes are red stones.
Paris
1809–1810
Length : 18 cm.
Inventory No.: 64.231
Tardy No. 192.
Analogue : M. G. Koolik : *Towers of
Spice*. Illustration No. 9

85 Spicebox
Silver, embossed. Originally a candle
snuffer and tray. The oblong tray
stands on four round legs, its rim is
rocaille. embossed. The box on the
scissors snuffer has embossed decoration.
"I.S." (Johann Seidel) mark on the
scissors
Viennese hallmark (1836) and "KP"
mark on the tray
Length of tray : 25 cm.
Inventory No.: 64.215. 1–2
Reitzner No. 1287

86 Spicebox
Partially gilt silver, filigree in the shape
of a prayerbook with clasp. It is dec-
orated with gray enamel and a blue
gem set in flowers on top.
No mark
Hungarian (?) Mid-19th century
Height: 7 cm.
Length 4.5 cm.
Width: 3 cm.
Inventory No.: 64.217

86

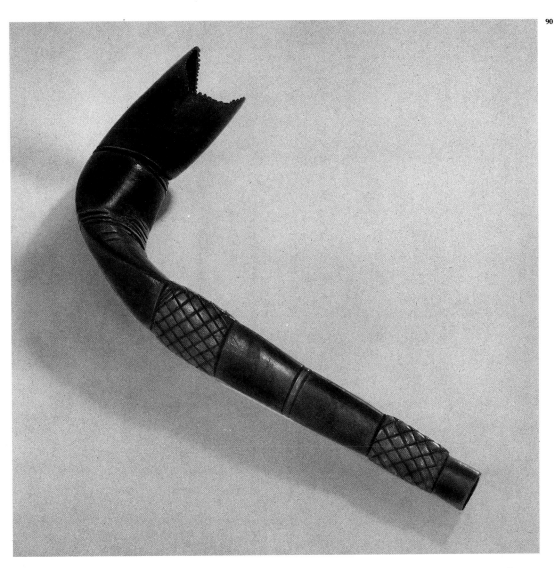

87 Spicebox
Brass, openwork, cast, in the shape of
a gondola, body of the boat is open-
work, with a little movable door and
two oarsmen.
No mark
Venice (?)
Late 19th century
Length: 17 cm.
Inventory No.: 64.2628

88 Spicebox
Silver, cast in the shape of a cow. On
the back that can be opened, a bee.
No mark
Eastern Europe
Second half of the 19th century
Length: 11 cm.
Inventory No.: 64.188

89 Spicebox
Silver filigree in the shape of a small
locomotive with four wheels and two
chimneys.
"E.L." initials
Óbuda (?)
Second half of the 19th century
Length: 7 cm.
Inventory No.: 64.225
Analogue: M. G. Koolik: *Towers of
Spice*. Illustration No. 14

90 Shofar
Black, carved of horn.
No mark
Tunisia (?)
Early 19th century
Length: 36 cm.
Inventory No.: 64.874

Analogue: K. Katz.—P. P. Kahane—
M. Broschi: *From the Beginning*. 195/c.

91 Honeypot with Cover

Porcelain, gilt, with small green leaf garlands. Hebrew inscription painted in gold frame, "Happy New Year". On the bottom, "G" mark with arrow.
Bohemian (Giesshübl)
Mid-19th century
Height : 10.5 cm.
Base : 7.5 cm.
Inventory No.: 64.870
Ilona P. Brestyánszky : *Ismerjük meg a kerámiát* [An Introduction to Ceramics]. No. 911

92 Tallit Clasp

Silver, embossed, engraved. Oblong shape. Two crowned heraldic lions holding the Torah crown and a shield between them in a frame of laurel wreath. The shield's inscription is faded.
Vienna
Viennese tax stamp (1807–1824)
19th century
Length : 11 cm.
Width : 8 cm.
Inventory No.: 64.869
Reitzner 132

93 Plate

Pewter, cast, engraved. Relief scene of Succoth (Tabernacles) in the middle. On the wavy rim with a double row of beads is the engraved Hebrew inscription, "In booths shall you dwell for seven days" (Leviticus 23 :42).
Based on Bernard Picart's etching
No mark
German
19th century
Height : 4.5 cm.
Diameter : 25 cm.
Inventory No.: 64.337

92

93

94 Etrog Container
(Cup with Cover)

Gilt silver, embossed, engraved. On the cylindrical body, the bust of "Solon, Cyrus rex, Pythagoras" in three medallions. Between them are fruit and leaf decorations. The cover has a fruit and leaf garland and a ball for the handle. The blessing for Lulav and Etrog is engraved on it, as well as the Hebrew inscription: "This cup belongs to the Hevrah Kaddishah Ner Tamid in Kanizsa".
Augsburg hallmark and "FTD" mark
17th century
Height: 17 cm.
Lip: 11.5 cm.
Inventory No.: 64.347

95 Etrog Container
(Tray with Handles)

Partially gilt silver, embossed. Acanthus and poppy garland on the inside, stylized leaves on the rim. The two handles are rocaille. Running around on the side is the inscription—engraved later—"This tray belongs to the Bikkur Holim Society of Kanizsa, made (?) in 564 [1804], to the minor reckoning".
Worn mark cs
Transylvania, Nagyszeben (?)
German (?)
17th century
Height: 3.2 cm.
Diameter: 20 cm.
Inventory No.: 64.342

95

96 Etrog Container

Silver, chased. Oval, embossed sugar bowl with cover. Engraved Hebrew inscription on top, "The gift of Moses Grünholz and his wife, Dverl, in the year 606 [1846] according to the minor reckoning".
Viennese hallmark (1744) and I.A. Kölbel's mark
Height: 7.5 cm.
Diameter: 12.5 cm.
Inventory No.: 64.336
Reitzner No. 650

97 Etrog Container
(Sugar Box)

Silver, embossed. Amor sharpening his arrow and Hebrew inscriptions on the attached oblong cover. Can be locked with a key. The engraved Hebrew inscription: "Acquired by the officers in Óbuda in the year of 595 [1835] according to the minor reckoning, for the holiday of Succoth" (Tabernacles).
Buda hallmark (1833) and József Károly Gretschl, Sr's mark
Height: 7 cm.
Length: 14.5 cm.
Width: 9 cm.
Inventory No.: 64.345
Kőszeghy Nos. 354, 315; *P. Brestyánszky* Nos. 56, 25
Exhibited: Exhibition of Applied Art in Old Buda and Pest. No. 42

98 Etrog Container
(Coconut Shell Cup)

Silver, framed in bands. Silver lip and legs. On the body engraved scenes in six fields. On top of the arched cover is a molded bird. On the rim is the engraved inscription, "Hayim Jacob, Samuel's son, Kiev, 660 [1900] according to the minor reckoning". The benediction for Lulav and Etrog is on the side.
No mark
Kiev
1900
Height: 13.5 cm.
Lip: 6.5 cm.
Inventory No.: 64.334

99 Hanukkah Lamp (Menorah)

Brass, cast. Stands on three animal paws. The baluster stem is round, the upper part is formed of stylized garlands with eight oil lamps on top. A heraldic crowned eagle rises out of the middle of the cruse. The ninth little lamp is also shaped like a jug.

No mark
Polish
17th century
Height: 73 cm.
Diameter: 23.5 cm.
Inventory No.: 77.1
Originally, it belonged to Chief Rabbi

Koppel Reich (1838–?)
Exhibited: Treasures of Ecclesiastical Collections. No. 371

100 Hanukkah Lamp

Brass, cast. The round baluster base is held up by three lions and three columns. The ringed stem has many divisions and four pairs of removable branches decorated with a lion each on a stylized garland. At the end of each branch is an oil lamp in the shape of a vase. On top of the stem sits a lion with shield. The ninth lamp is on its head. Towards the center of the can-

delabrum is the Hebrew inscription, "The seven lamps shall give light" (Moses IV, 8:2). Around the base, the inscription, "Donated by the virtuous lady Baile, the daughter of the scholar Solomon in the Holy Society of Lemberg".

No mark
Polish
Harry G. Friedman Collection No. 145
Around 1700
Height: 125 cm.
Inventory No.: 64.1168
Kayser op. cit. No. LXXII

101 Hanukkah Lamp
Brass, cast. The base rises out of three lions that are connected to the Menorah by winged serpents. Above the base, at the divisions of the stem, there are two wreaths with eight arms with flowers. Above them four arms on both sides topped by a vase-shape candle holder. In front, on the arm reaching forward, is the ninth candle holder. Between the arms, in the center, are two prancing lions. Above them a crown and Polish eagle. At the base of the standing eagle is a Hebrew inscription (of the benediction).
No mark
Polish
17th century
Height : 190 cm.
Diameter : 56 cm.
Inventory No. : 64.1167
Narkiss No. LXII, No. 181

102 Hanukkah Lamp
Copper, cast. A halberdier on each side and the bust of Emperor Joseph II on the back, between four lions. Eight oil pans on the tray.
No mark
Bohemia
Late 18th century
Height : 11 cm.
Length : 25 cm.
Inventory No. : 64.259

103 Hanukkah Lamp
Copper, cast. Eight oil pans on the bench. The covers of the pans are fish-shaped. The back is openwork with two deer, garlands and two doves on top. There is a lion on each side holding a candlestick with its upright tail.
No mark
Eastern Europe
18th century
Height : 24 cm.
Length : 26 cm.
Inventory No. : 64.269

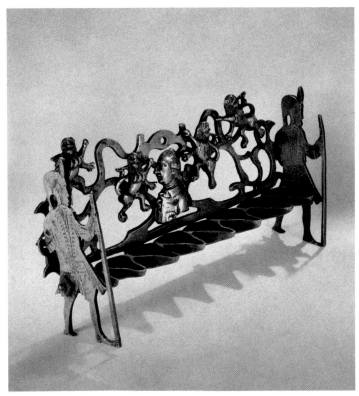

104

105

104 Hanukkah Lamp

Brass, cast. It stands on four bent legs. On its bench are eight square oil pans. In the middle of the back is openwork foliation with lyres. The sides are S-shaped. The holder for the ninth lamp is on the right side.
No mark
Eastern Europe (?)
Mid-19th century
Height : 18 cm.
Length : 26 cm.
Inventory No.: 64.272

105 Hanukkah Lamp

Brass, cast. It has round wooden legs. The tall back has four rows of openwork holes. On top center a half-round palmette and the bust of Napoleon. Eight oil pans on the bench (the legs are a later addition).
No mark
Polish
Early 19th century
Length : 28 cm.
Inventory No.: 64.262

106 Hanukkah Lamp

Bronze, cast. The bench is made up of eight square oil lamps. The openwork back has two prancing lions and garlands, with a fruit bowl in the middle. The ninth oil pan sits on the head of one of the lions.
No mark
Italy
16th century
Height : 19 cm.
Length : 21 cm.
Inventory No.: 64.308
Narkiss No. VI, No. 19

107 Hanukkah Lamp

Brass, cast. Under the roof, the back has the form of a temple with an open arcade. The bench has an openwork balustrade in front with eight vase-shaped oil pans. The back plate with its cutout windows and door next to which are candlesticks is reminiscent of a synagogue. Over the roof are two stylized animals and a rampant lion on each sidepanel with a candlestick on the tail.
No mark
Polish
Early 19th century
Height : 28 cm.
Length : 36 cm.
Inventory No.: 64.300
Weinstein op. cit. 132, No. 165

106

107

108 Hanukkah Lamp
Silver, cast, embossed, pierced with filigree. "Baal Shem Tov" type, named after the founder of Hassidism who by tradition owned one of this type. It stands on six bent legs. Eight oil pans in the shape of jugs on the bench. The two sides and back have filigree work with openwork foliate design. Torah decoration representing a miniature Ark with bird on the two sides and a little door that can be opened in the center. On top is a crown with three hoops and bird. The bench is checkered. On one side, a servant light. The other sevant light is missing.
Number 12 quality mark and a hallmark in the shape of a deer.
Polish
Early 19th century
Height : 22 cm.
Length : 29.5 cm.
Inventory No. : 64.286
Weinstein No. 172

109 Hanukkah Lamp
Lead. Cast in the form of eight chairs.
No mark
Polish

Around 1915
Height : 7.6 cm.
Length : 14.5 cm.
Width : 3 cm.
Inventory No. : 64.326
Narkiss No. 111

110 Hanukkah Lamp
Silver, cast. The four legs are winged lion heads. The base has openwork foliate design and a palmette frieze. Eight shell-shape oil pans on the bench. Two horns of plenty with pomegranate on the canopied cartouche-shaped back. Under the canopy there is an antique urn in a vine wreath.

No mark
Austrian or Hungarian
Around 1830
Height : 35 cm.
Length : 30.5 cm.
Inventory No. : 64.277

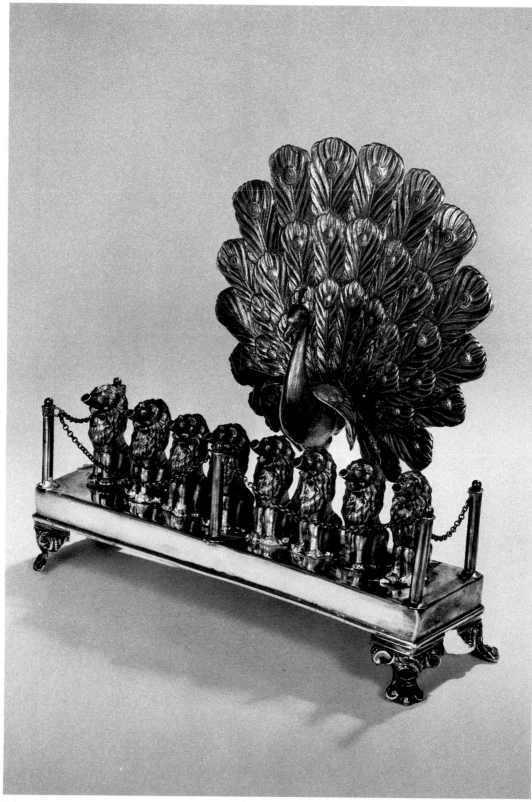

111 Hanukkah Lamp
Silver, cast, embossed. The flat bench stands on rocaille-ornamented legs. The oil pans are eight sitting lions. On the back, in the center, is a peacock with spread tail.
Viennese hallmark (1860) in the back and "F.T." mark
Height: 26 cm.
Length: 24.5 cm.
Inventory No.: 64.282

112 Hanukkah Lamp
Silver, cast. It stands on two triangular legs with openwork leaves and flowers on them. Cut out palmette-decorated frieze on the back and eight small spoon-shaped oil pans on the bench. A lyre and two swans in the center of the back. The servant light is on the side at the top.
Óbuda hallmark (1864) and Fülöp (Philip) Adler's trademark
Height: 11 cm.
Length: 26 cm.
Width: 5.5 cm.
Inventory No.: 64.284
Kőszeghy No. 375; *P. Brestyánszky* No. 98

113 Pair of Candlesticks
Silver, pressed metal. Eightfold curved and ribbed base. The baluster stem is decorated with leaves, roses and pomegranate flowers. The candle holder is ribbed, the holder is in the shape of a goblet.
Viennese hallmark (1863) and "Reiner" mark
Height: 30.5 cm.
Diameter of base: 14 cm.
Inventory No.: 80.10. 1–2

114 Megillah Case
Silver, chased. Ribbed and embossed base and top with knop in the shape of a pineapple. Acanthus leaf decoration and Hebrew inscription on the cylindrical body.

Viennese hallmark (1844) and Adam Hügel's mark
Length : 20.5 cm.
Diameter : 3 cm.
Inventory No. : 64.2627
Reitzner No. 1378

115 Pair of Candlesticks
Silver, cast, embossed, pressed Chased bouquet of roses on the eight-fold, curved base, baluster stem. The candle holder is goblet shaped with a movable molded pheasant on top.
Viennese mark (1858) and Carl Schill's mark
Height : 37 cm.
Diameter of base : 16.5 cm.
Inventory No. : 64.23. 1–2
Reitzner No. 1228

114

116 Purim Tray

Pewter, cast, engraved. In the center, Purim scene with Haman leading the mounted Mordecai. Around the scene are pomegranate and tulip engraved decorations. Hebrew inscription on both sides of the rim, "From the synagogue of Baja [?]".
No mark
Southern Germany (?)
1768
Diameter: 21 cm.
Inventory No.: 64.359

117 Purim Tray

Pewter, cast, engraved. In the center, Purim scene of Haman leading the mounted Mordecai. Hebrew quotation from the Book of Esther is engraved on the rim, "Then took Haman the apparel and the horse, and arrayed Mordecai and caused him to ride through the street of the city . . ." (6:11). On the bottom is the first letter of the Hebrew alphabet, the Aleph (the maker's name?) and "ISI" initials.
Hungarian (?)
Late 18th century, early 19th century
Diameter: 30 cm.
Inventory No.: 64.360

118 Seder Plate
(Plate V)

Turned, tinglazed majolica with Biblical scenes painted in high temperature colors. There are Biblical figures in four heart-shaped medallions, with tiny multicolored flowers between them. Hebrew text in the middle, Verse 1 of Psalm 113, "Praise, O ye servants of the Lord". Under the Psalm are instructions for the conduct of the Seder. There is also the inscription, "Jacob the Cohen of Altona". The letters "KT" in Hebrew and a crown in black paint on the bottom (which was probably added at a later date).
Italian
1654
Diameter: 47 cm.
Inventory No.: 64.427
Bibliography: B. C. Roth, *Jewish Art.* Tel Aviv, 1961
Exhibited: Treasures of Ecclesiastical Collections. No. 394. Analogues in the Jewish Museum of Prague, London, New York and Paris

120

119 Seder Plate
(Plate VI)

Turned, tinglazed majolica painted in high temperature colors. On the rim, four larger and four smaller stylized heart-shaped medallions with the figures of Moses, Aaron, David and Solomon. Two large medallions bear illustrations of Isaac blessing Jacob and the selling of Joseph. The other two have flower bouquets. The Hebrew inscription in the center is the text of Psalm 114 and "Jakob Azulai Peśaro, 1652".

Blue "JA" mark on the bottom
Italian (Pesaro?)
1652 (?)
Diameter: 48 cm.
Inventory No.: 64.445
Bibliography: B. C. Roth, *Jewish Art*. 342
Exhibited: Treasures of Ecclesiastical Collections. No. 394

120 Seder Plate

Earthenware, painted in blue and ribbed edge. In the middle, the portrait of Marcus Benedictus, the famous Talmud scholar, and his name in Latin characters. "PÁPA" stamped on the bottom.
Pápa (Hungary)
1837–1839
Diameter: 22.4 cm.
Inventory No.: 64.423
Bibliography: "Néhai Kilényi Pál gyűjteménye" (The Late Pál Kilényi's Collection). *A Gyűjtő* V (1916). No. 313

121 Seder Plate

Porcelain, with hand-painted decoration. The scalloped rim is colored lilac and has white wreath of leaves. Inside, in oval medallions are instructions for the conduct of the Seder in black Hebrew letters. In the center, three colored roses.
Herend
Mid-19th century
Diameter: 35 cm.
Inventory No.: 64.418

122 Seder Plate

Porcelain. Hand-painted, basket-weave rim. In the middle, on a white field, lilac-and-red rose wreath and the text of *Ha Lahma*. In the blue field below the rim are the elements of the Seder celebration in eight oval frames.
Herend
Mid-19th century
Diameter: 24 cm.
Inventory No.: 64.420

122

123 Seder Plate

Earthenware. Illustration of the "Wise Son" in sepia after the Amsterdam Haggadah's Haham. The word "Haham" in Hebrew under the picture. The mark "PÁPA" on the bottom.
Pápa
1837–1839
Diameter: 24 cm.
Inventory No.: 64.443

124 Seder Plate

Porcelain. Hand-painted. Lilac-tinted, rose-colored flowers and leaves alternate each other on the green rim. In Hebrew, elements of the Seder ceremony in eight medallions inside the plate. In two medallions, the names of Simon Steiner and Antónia Steiner. A bouquet of flowers in the middle of the plate.
Herend
Mid-19th century
Diameter: 31 cm.
Inventory No.: 64.422

125 Seder Tray
Earthenware, hand-painted. On the oval rim, openwork rosettes and raised wreaths. Inside, in oval medallions, texts referring to the Seder ceremony. In the center is the text of *Ha Lahma*, framed in bouquets of roses and a garland.
Herend
Around 1840
Diameter: 24 cm.
Inventory No.: 64.419

126 Seder Plate
(Plate VII/a)
Porcelain. Hand-painted and gilt. On the peacock blue scaly rim in six white frames are the Hebrew instructions for the conduct of the Seder. In the middle, the picture of the celebrating family of five persons, with the scene of the washing of hands.
Herend
Mid-19th century
Diameter: 33 cm.
Inventory No.: 64.426
Exhibited: Treasures of Ecclesiastical Collections. No. 935

127 Seder Plate
(Plate VII/b)
Porcelain. Hand-painted. On its wavy rim, in eight green medallions are the elements of the Seder celebration in Hebrew. In the middle of the rose-colored field is an illustration of a celebrating family consisting of six members.
Herend
Mid-19th century
Diameter: 33 cm.
Inventory No.: 64.425.

125

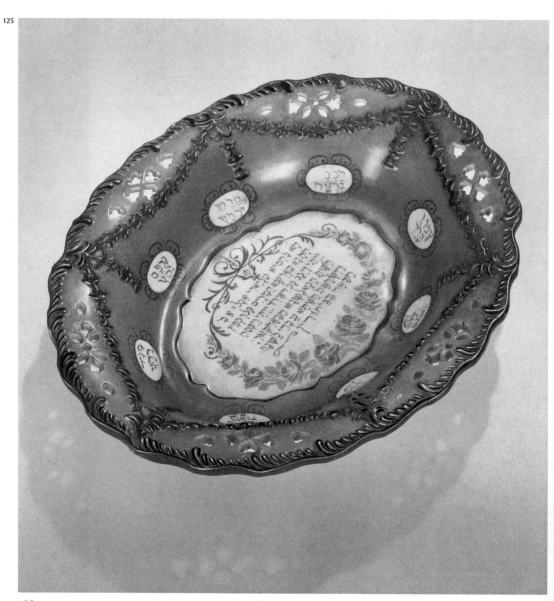

128 Seder Tray (with Stand)

Porcelain. Hand-painted. Rosettes in radiating geometric design. Between them, in medallions, are instructions for the conduct of the Seder. The text of the introduction to the Haggadah, "This is the bread of affliction [Ha Lahma]", in Hebrew letters, is in the middle of the tray. The painted inscription at the bottom, "Vilmos Fischer's workshop of porcelain painting, Kolozsvár, 1881".
Diameter: 36.5 cm.
Inventory No.: 64.417

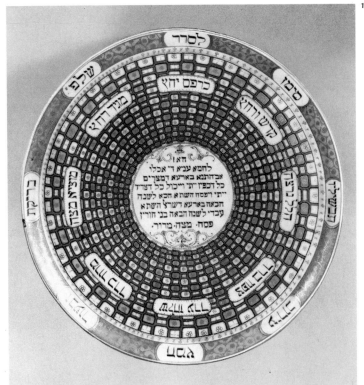

129

129 Seder Plate

Porcelain. Painted. Lavishly gilt. Kubasch patterned. Elements of the Seder celebration on the rim. The text of *Ha Lahma* in the middle.
Vilmos Fischer
Kolozsvár
1896
Diameter: 39 cm.
Inventory No.: 64.416

130 Seder Plate
(Plate VIII/a)

Porcelain with gilt stand. Hand-painted. Gold leaf and berry ornamentation on the wavy rim. All around, the painted symbols of Pass-

over in red ribboned frame: lamb, Passover (Paschal) lamb, Matzah, bitter herbs, in Hebrew. In the middle, Biblical scene in red: Moses calming the sea. The Hebrew text around it is, "Remember, you were slaves in Egypt" (Deuteronomy, 24:22).
Painted by Jónás Neumann
Nyitra
Late 19th century
Diameter: 39 cm.
Inventory No.: 64.449.

131 Seder Plate
(Plate VIII/b)

Porcelain, hand-painted. In the middle, on a white field, two bouquets of

flowers arranged asymmetrically, with two single flowers painted in natural colors between them. Above, painted in black, the Hebrew for egg, roast, bitter herb, Harosset (a mixture of cinnamon, apples and nuts) and greens.
Painted by Jónás Neumann
Nyitra
Late 19th century
Diameter: 37 cm.
Inventory No.: 64.448

132 Tiered Seder Tray

Turned wood. Four round, flat trays supported by upright balusters and legs. Five little cup-shaped receptacles with legs on top.
Hungarian
Mid-19th century
Height : 39 cm.
Diameter : 29 cm.
Inventory No. : 66.52

133 Goblet

Porcelain. Hand-painted portrait of Vilmos Farkasházy Fischer's father in gilt medallion. The Hungarian inscription on the bottom, "As a souvenir, Vilmos Fischer in Kolozsvár, 1879".

No mark
Height : 26 cm.
Base : 5.5 cm.
Inventory No. : 64.428

134 Seder Cup
Golden-brown lead crystal, polished.
Etched scene of the Seder, with
Hebrew inscription on the back.
No mark
Bohemian
Mid-19th century
Height : 13.8 cm.
Base : 6.5 cm.
Inventory No. : 64.429

135 Wine Flask
Glass, molded, with etched Seder
scene and "Pessah" etched in Hebrew.
"NI" initials in a leaf garland. Inscribed,
"Zum Andenken 1860".
Hungarian
Height : 14.5 cm.
Inventory No. : 64.522

136 Seder Plate
Pewter, cast, engraved. In the middle, an engraved double-headed, crowned heraldic griffin. Inscribed on the rim are the elements of the Seder celebration. On the bottom, the inscription "17 SCHLAKA 59", and three tin stamps with roses.
Bohemian
1759
Diameter: 35.5 cm.
Inventory No.: 64.834

137 Seder Plate
Pewter, cast, engraved. In the rim, the flowering branch of a tree and the Hebrew inscription of the order of Seder ceremony, and the year 526 [1766] according to the minor reckoning. In the middle, "Wolf" in Hebrew letters.
Eastern Europe
Tin stamp "1766" with rosette
Diameter: 30 cm.
Inventory No.: 64.535

138 Seder Plate (two pieces)

Pewter, cast, engraved. On the wavy, contoured rim are engraved Hebrew abbreviations. On the bottom, "MT" mark with crown and "F. EVERS" stamp with two angels, a wreath and lion head. The second piece is its pair.
F. Evers
English (?)
Mid-18th century
Diameter: 25 cm.
Inventory No.: 64.548. 1—2

139 Seder Plate

Pewter, cast, engraved. Seder scene in the middle. Hebrew engraved quotation on the rim, "And thus shall you eat it: with your loins girded, your shoes on your feet, and your staff in your hand; and you shall eat it in haste—it is the Lord's passover" (Exodus, 12:11). There is also the Mogen David—the Star of David. On the bottom, the initials "C. W." and a stamp on an angel with flag and scales.
German or Tyrolean
18th century
Diameter: 36 cm.
Inventory No.: 64.836

140

141

140 Seder Plate
Pewter, cast, engraved. Engraved on the rim are the elements of the Seder celebration in Hebrew and "SE" initials. "GB" initials engraved on the bottom.
Bohemian
Late 18th century, early 19th century
Diameter : 30 cm.
Inventory No. : 64.547

141 Seder Plate
Pewter, cast, engraved. Inside the plate is an engraved scene with two lions, one tower; under them the Ark of the Torah and "1819" engraved in Latin characters. Engraved on the rim are the elements of the Seder celebration in Hebrew. On the bottom, three tin stamps with roses and "CHLAHA" mark in oblong frame.
Hungarian (?)
1819
Diameter : 38 cm
Inventory No. : 64.845

142 Seder Plate
Pewter, cast, engraved. Engraved Biblical scene in the middle : David and Goliath with Hebrew inscription and floriate design. Engraved on the rim are elements of the Seder celebration in Hebrew. On the bottom is engraved "Josephus Adler Anno 1829" and the Hebrew initials "DM".
Hungarian (?)
1829
Diameter : 34 cm.
Inventory No. : 64.849

143

144

143 Book of Psalms with Commentary

In silver binding. High embossed Biblical (?) scenes on both sides. Acanthus foliate decoration on the spine. Provided with silver clasps.
No mark
Amsterdam (?)
17th century
Height: 11.8 cm.
Width: 7.3 cm.
Inventory No.: 64. 685

144 Prayerbook

In claret velvet binding, silver overlay, openwork acanthus garlands. On the cover, in oval field surrounded by a wreath, is the name of the owner, Abraham Mordecai, son of Gumpel-flesch, engraved. Above that is a five-pointed coronet.
Hannover-Altstadt hallmark (1696) and "A" mark
Height: 19.3 cm.
Width: 12.5 cm.
Inventory No.: 64.686
Rosenberg No. 2489

145 Rabbi Lipót Lőw's Bible

Bound in silver, embossed, chased. Decorated with stylized foliage and flowers. Embossed on the cover is a lion couchant. On the back is a heart with the engraved Hebrew inscription, "Keepsake from all who love excellence. Pápa, 1850". With a clasp.
Viennese hallmark (1850) and "AW" (Louis Vaugoin) monogram
Height: 17 cm.
Width: 11 cm.
Inventory No.: 64.612
Reitzner No. 1423

145

146 Prayerbook with Commentary
Bound in brown velvet. Silver filigree
palmette mountings, one big and one
small rosette in the middle.
The clasp has a "GS" mark and a "13"
hallmark stamp. GS (György Sodom-
ka) master
Nyitra
Mid-19th century
Height : 24 cm.
Width : 13 cm.
Inventory No.: 71.5
Kőszeghy No. 1585

147 Sephardi Holiday Prayerbook (Mahzor)

For the Pilgrimage Holiday. Open-work silver mounting, thick with acanthus garlands, on brown velvet base. In the middle of the binding, on a pointed shield is the date 604 [1844] and the engraved name of the owner, Jacob, on the other side. Embossed leaf decoration on the spine.
Viennese
1844
Height : 18 cm.
Width : 12 cm.
Inventory No. : 64.684

148 Prayerbook

Green velvet binding, ivory decoration with cutout flowers, silver mountings. In the center in the front are the two Tablets of the Law in an oval field. Provided with clasps.
No mark
Viennese
Around 1880
Height : 17.5 cm.
Width : 12.2 cm.
Inventory No. : 64.806

149 Prayerbook (Siddur)

With German translation. Undressed pigskin binding, silver mountings. Blue and white enamel tulip decoration on the front cover. Intertwined "MW" enameled initials in an oval field. Two enameled clasps. (Engagement gift.)
Budapest
1889
Height : 18 cm.
Width : 13 cm.
Inventory No.: 64.789

150 Prayerbook

Ivory binding, gilt silver mounting. Decorative intertwined ivory "JHES" initials on the front cover. The clasp is engraved with flower decoration. The silver engraved scrollwork bears the inscription, "Pest, 4 Dec., 1870".
Pest
1870
Height : 18 cm.
Width : 13 cm.
Inventory No.: 64.609

151 Prayerbook

For Israelites, in Hungarian translation. Red velvet, ivory mounted de luxe binding. On the front, a neo-Gothic cell (stylized Ark of the Torah) with the two Tablets of the Law and Torah crown above. Stylized cut out garland below the cell. Metal clasps.
No mark
Viennese
1894
Height : 18.5 cm.
Width : 12 cm.
Inventory No.: 76.1

150

151

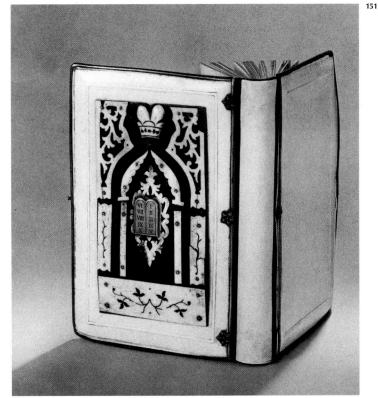

152 Prayerbook

Brown leather binding with mother-of-pearl and metal mounting. On the front cover, on top to the right, the two Tablets of the Law on mother-of-pearl mounting and at the bottom, to the left, is a Torah Scroll with floriate design. On the spine is the gilt inscription, "Die Himmelspforte" [The Gate of Heaven] (D. M. Letteris. Bp., 1890, V. Lôwy's Sohn.) Metal clasp.
Hungarian
1890
Height : 18.3 cm.
Width : 12.5 cm.
Inventory No. : 64.807

153 Prayerbook

Tefillat Yisrael (Israel's Prayer) with German translation. The binding is pigskin in natural color. The four corners of the front cover are decorated with stylized colored flowers in enamel. In the middle in ogival medallion intertwined "IEB" initials under a five-point coronet with a little forget-me-not under it. The clasp, too, has enamel decoration.
Viennese
About 1883
Height : 18.5 cm.
Width : 13 cm.
Inventory No. : 64.801

154 Tefillin Boxes (two pieces)

Silver, embossed, engraved. Two cubes
on bent square base. Can be closed.
Stylized rosette engraved on top.
Lemberg tax stamp at the bend
(1806–1807)
Polish
Height : 7 cm.
Width : 5 cm.
Inventory No. : 64.741. 1–2
Reitzner 129, No. 133
Analogue : *Synagoga*. No. 278

155 Hanging Amulet

Silver, cartouche shaped, embossed, cast, with openwork. A baroque curved and bent acanthus leaf on each side with "C" scrolls. Crest with eagle in the middle. A bunch of grapes at the bottom. A censer on the left above the acanthus leaf, and a high priest's mitre, on clouds, in the middle. Canopy with bunched ribbon on top. On the back, on the upper left, a seven-branched Menorah. To the right, the two Tablets of the Law.

On both sides in the middle, the Hebrew text "Eternal".

No mark
Italian

Mid-18th century
Height : 12 cm.
Polish
Inventory No.: 64.564
Analogue : V. A. Klagsbald : *Jewish Treasures from Paris*. No. 163; *Synagoga*, No. 443

156 Amulet

Silver, cast, engraved. Shaped like the Ark of the Torah, a column on each side, neo-baroque decoration at the edges. Engraved in the middle is the Hebrew text of the blessing.

No mark
Austrian or Hungarian
First half on the 19th century

Height : 8.5 cm.
Width : 5 cm.
Inventory No.: 64.578

157 Amulet

Silver, embossed, engraved. Inside the square field topped by a three-lobed arch are two crowned twisted columns. Between them is the Hebrew letter "H" above which is another crown.

No mark
Austrian or Hungarian
Late 18th century
Height : 7.3 cm.
Width : 5.7 cm.
Inventory No.: 64.573

155

158 Amulet

Silver, embossed. Louis XVI cartouche-shaped rim with weave-pattern ornaments. Divided into two parts. In the lower field between two twisted columns is a Biblical scene: the Sacrifice of Isaac. In the upper part, among clouds, a book opened at the Ten Commandments, with a coronet above it. On the back, a Menorah with "Eternal" in Hebrew and the first words of the Priestly Blessing.
Rome hallmark
Italian
Late 18th century
Height: 8.5 cm.
Width: 5.2 cm.
Inventory No.: 64.574
Rosenberg No. 7433

159 Amulet
Silver filigree in the shape of a prayer-book with clasp. On the front and back, in a round medallion, the Hebrew inscription, "Eternal".
No mark
Hungarian
Early 19th century
Height : 7.5 cm.

Width : 5.5 cm.
Inventory No. : 64.562

160 Amulet
Partially gilt silver filigree. The cylindrical body is decorated with openwork leaves. On it are four rings to hold a chain. There is a medallion at the end of the chain that opens. The cylinder has openwork semispherical heads at each end, one of which can be opened.
"ET" mark
Austro–Hungarian
19th century
Height : 11 cm.
Length of chain : 45 cm.
Inventory No. : 64.563

160

161 Circumcision Knife (Mohel Knife)
Silver. The mother-of-pearl handle is decorated with carved and engraved standing leaves. At the end is the figure of a crouching lion.
No mark
Hungarian (?)
Early 19th century
Length: 19 cm.
Inventory No.: 64.700

162 Circumcision Knife (Mohel Knife)
Silver. Filigree and palmette decorated handle with a knob at the end.
No mark
Hungarian (?)
First half of the 19th century
Length: 20 cm.
Inventory No.: 64.693

163 Sabbath Lamp

Brass, cast. Heavy baluster stem. The oil receptacle is a six-pointed star without drip bowl.
No mark
18th century
Height: 29 cm.
Inventory No.: 64.220
Weinstein 43, No. 19

164 Snuff Box

Inlaid mother-of-pearl. Oblong with cut off corners. Around the top, inside an engraved garland, is a Hebrew inscription. Rachel's tomb on one side, Jerusalem on the other—the Sanctuary and the Wailing Wall (Kotel). On the two sides, the Hebrew inscription, "Jerusalem, Wailing Wall", and "Souvenir, with love . . .".
No mark
Jerusalem
19th century
Height: 7.5 cm.
Width: 5 cm.
Inventory No.: 64.572

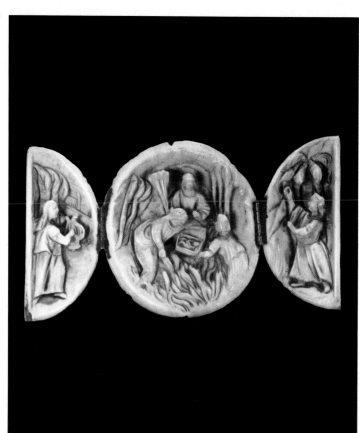

165 Ball
Ivory. Can be opened. Inside a carved
scene: "Finding of Moses".
No mark
German (?)
18th century.
Diameter: 5.5 cm.
Inventory No.: 64.606

166 Synagogue Seat Ticket
For Leopold Schwarcz. Paper. The
makeup is framed with etchings of
Biblical scenes. Printed German text in
the middle. Valid for the year
1845–1846.
"No. 52 L." seat number.
Pest
1845
Height: 14 cm.
Length: 9 cm.
Inventory No.: 64.823

166

TEXTILES

In Jewish religious cult, there is an important role for spectacularly ornamented textiles. Carpets, hangings, curtains are often mentioned with emphasis in the Hebrew Bible; God's House cannot be imagined without them. "Then all the skilled among those engaged in the work made the tabernacle of ten strips of cloth, which they made of fine twisted linen, blue, purple, and crimson yarns . . ." (Exodus 36 : 8). Similar to the hangings were also the curtains: "They made the curtain of blue, purple, and crimson yarns, and fine twisted linen . . . done in embroidery" (Exodus 36 : 35–37).

The rich, colorful embroidery that extended all over a given material was typical of fabrics in subsequent times as well. These decorations serve a double purpose. On the one hand, the symbols of Biblical events and commandments show the object's ritual use; on the other, the blank surfaces can reflect the style of the given era. The most spectacular pieces serve the cult of the Torah, as do the curtain for the Ark of the Torah, the cover for the lectern and the Torah mantle. These, depending on their use, are different in size but similar in execution—flat or raised embroidery with imitation precious stones and overlays on silk or velvet. The dominant ornament of the inside of the synagogue is the curtain on the Ark of the Torah. Its purpose, as is obvious by its name, is to hide the cabinet holding the Torah, the holiest of objects, from the eyes of the uninitiate. Its role is prominent in the Hebrew Bible where the tabernacle that Moses built is described: "And he brought the ark into the tabernacle . . . and screened the ark of the testimony; as the Lord commanded Moses" (Exodus 40 : 21). In ancient synagogues it was put in front of the apse; the Sephardim have the curtain inside the Ark, the Ashkenazim in front of it.

Generally, it was donated by the well-to-do in memory of their loved ones. Previously, the material often served another purpose—it had been the donor's wedding gown or other gala dress, or perchance the hangings of a household. These curtains are oblong in shape and their measure depends on the size of the Ark. They are hung by the upper end and the fastenings are often covered by a scalloped narrow valance. The oldest among the Ark curtains preserved in the world's various collections are from the 14th and 15th centuries. But the larger number is from the 17th century.[1]

In the 17th century and the beginning of the 18th century, the Ark curtains had flat embroidery on them. This was frequently two pillars with vine around them representing Solomon's Temple; a Torah crown held by two prancing lions—the symbols of Judah—in the center. Characteristically, ornamentation is predominant and religious symbols retreat into the background during the 18th century. Raised embroidery shines on velvet or silk—often brocade[2]—base. In the 19th-century pieces, a frame in contrasting color surrounds the stylized religious symbols: thin columns, lions, the drape showing the Tabernacle with the tablets of the Ten Commandments and other symbols contained in the makeup. The drapery of the 17th and 18th centuries is also decorated with symbols: the altar of the Jerusalem Sanctuary, the shield of the High Priest, the seven-branched Menorah, etc. With the passage of time, it becomes smooth and is decorated with tassels only. However, there are 19th-century examples where the valance is omitted and its arches are imitated by tassels.

In literature, the Torah often appears as a noble lady, as a queen—the Torah mantle is to adorn her. Its execution and decoration resemble those of the curtain of the Ark of the Torah. The two ivied columns, the two tablets of the Ten Commandments, the Lions of Judah and, of course, the crown are frequent.

The table on which the Torah Scroll is placed while it is being read is covered also with a similarly decorated cloth. Only one can be found in our collection and its exact use is doubtful. It may have been part of a curtain of the Ark of the Torah.

Beside the ornamentations, the three types of fabrics are also decorated with calligraphic inscriptions. These are usually Biblical quotations or particulars of the donors or those in whose memory the donation was made (the former we translate, the latter—because they are repetitious formulas and contain little information—we leave as is; we do supply the date of donation and give the name of the donor if it is of significance for some reason).

Of the holidays, the Seder evening celebration provides special opportunity for the use of fabrics, since the table and the trays are all covered. The Museum has several such Seder plate covers. Most of the time, the beginning of a Seder evening's prayer can be found on them. A cover of around 1880 has a form that is of special interest. Its pockets, placed one under the other, assist the course of the ritual meal (No. 187).

Special importance is given the Mizrah (East) tablets in the house of devout families. Certain prayers have to be recited facing Jerusalem. Therefore, the eastern wall of the house has to be marked.

When making our selection, the artistic points of view were not the main criteria. If they had been, the painted red flag (No. 188), which is the Yiddish-language document of the 1905 Russian Revolution and, as such, is a genuine historical rarity, would have had to be omitted. As a curiosity, selected also was a bonnet that was worn by the mothers-in-law at weddings (No. 190). On first inspection, it appears to be Near Eastern or rather from the south. But, knowing a similar example in Nyitra, it can be considered part of national costume of the highlands, probably made popular by its Oriental appearance despite its lack of ties to Jewish tradition.

Generally, we can observe two tendencies in fabrics of the collection. One group was specifically made for religious purposes, even if the material had once fulfilled another function. In the objects of a smaller group, the religious character fades into the background and the piece that had originally a different objective retains its form (as, for instance, the Turkish Seder plate cover, No. 185, from the Balkans).

In both cases, dating is extraordinarily difficult. Even if there is a date in the embroidered text, it may not be indicative of the year in which the object was made. The 19th-century pieces were often made of 18th-century silk (Nos. 168, 172, 175, 177, 180). Certain motifs of an earlier style of embroidery were also preserved and copied. A characteristic example of this is a curtain of the Ark of the Torah (No. 173) made in 1818 whose style is of no later time than the last third of the 18th century, while some of its arabesque motifs recall 17th-century Spanish art. At the same time, the piece itself is probably older than the date of the inscription because the text is a later addition. Furthermore, the fact that the fabric had already been embroidered when it was cut and put together proves that it had a different purpose originally.

The influence of the style of an era manifests itself in a specially interesting way in our country where, in the course of the 16th and 17th centuries, a very high quality embroidery had developed as the amalgamation of Western—mainly Italian Renaissance and Near Eastern (Turkish) art. We call this type of embroidery with colored silk and metal thread on silk or linen "domestic" embroidery to distinguish it from the simpler, but in many aspects similar, 18th to 19th-century peasant embroidery which is mainly on home-made material.

The influence of this peculiarly Hungarian art of embroidery from the territory of historical Hungary is indicated in two pieces from our collection. According to its inscription, one is a curtain of the Ark of the Torah and valance (No. 167) from 1742. This is a very interesting piece from the point of view of dating because the valance is made of contrasting material and could not be of a later date than the 17th century, which is also the case with analogues. But the curtain itself does not follow the analogues because it has the typical motifs of "domestic" embroidery, a garland of pomegranates, tulips, fields of flowers, etc. Though some of its parts and the composition of the frame is of the 17th century, the abundant ornamentation of the makeup and the daintier and thinner lines would make dating it in the 18th century more acceptable. A Seder plate cover (No. 184) causes just as much racking of the researcher's brain. Considering both its material and motifs, it could be counted as an example of domestic embroidery and, as such, it assumes special significance because of pomegranate and tulip garlands framing the symbols of the Seder ceremony. At the same time, it is a good example of continued attachment to fashion, because the material and the motifs are characteristic of the 17th century, while the colors and the crowded composition indicate the 18th century.

The pieces of the collection can also be divided into two groups according to the standard of their technique. The larger part shows high quality craftsmanship and is the work of professional craftsmen. We even know who made some of them (No. 169, Kálmán Grünwald; No. 176, Károly Grünwaldt). The designer of the latter is identical with the architect of the Dohány utca Synagogue, Ludwig Förster. These curtains were designed together with the constituent parts of the building, which also shows the importance of fabrics. A smaller, very charming group of items is female needlework. The execution and decoration of these are similar to the fabrics used in households and are expressive of the fashion of the era.

NOTES

1. R. Krüger: *Die Kunst der Synagoge*, Leipzig, 1968. 52–53
2. CIETA (Centre International d'Etudes des Textiles Anciens), the international organization dealing with the history of textiles, does not recommend the use of "brocade" because the word does not refer to technique. It recommends the use of "Lampas" instead. Comp. Emőke László's study entitled "Művészi szövetneműek" [Artistic Textiles]. In: Pál Voit (Ed.) *Régiségek könyve* [Book of Antiquities], Budapest, 1983. 295

SELECTED BIBLIOGRAPHY

Cohn—Wiener, E.: *Die jüdische Kunst. Ihre Geschichte von Anfängen bis zur Gegenwart*, Berlin, 1929

Judaica. Kölnisches Stadtmuseum, bearbeitet von L. Franzheim, Köln, 1980

Krüger, R.: *Die Kunst der Synagoge. Eine Einführung in die Probleme von Kunst und Kult des Judentums*, Leipzig, 1968

Landsberger, F.: *A History of Jewish Art*, Cincinnati, 1946

Monumenta Judaica, 2000 Jahre Geschichte und Kultur am Rhein, Ausstellungskatalog, Köln, 1963–1964

Roth, R.: *Jewish Art, An Illustrated History*, Tel Aviv, 1961

Roth, R.: *Die Kunst der Juden*, Frankfurt am Main, 1963

Volávková, H.: *The Jewish Museum of Prague*, Prague, 1968

Volávková, H.: *The Synagogue Treasures of Bohemia and Moravia*, Prague, 1949

167 Curtain of the Ark of the Torah (Parohet) and Valance (Kapporet)

The valance is red velvet with silver thread. It is flat embroidered with geometric stitches. The curtain is mustard-yellow and red velvet, flat and applied work with geometrically stitched green silk and silver thread. The upper end of the curtain is fringe trimmed.

The valance has the shape of an irregular pentagon. Four of its corners are curved fields, at the two sides are a closed crown each, then a Renaissance vase with carnation and pomegranate design. Two eagles, their wings spread, face each other in the center. Above them is a closed crown. The valance's fifth, straight side, i. e., the bottom, has attached to it a sevenfold shield. On the length of the valance, in garlanded frames, are the emblems of the altar in the Jerusalem Sanctuary and their Hebrew names. The first and seventh have the High Priest's Breast-plate, the second has the seven-branched Menorah, the third has the altar aflame, in the middle are the two Tablets of the Ten Commandments with five lines each of the first words of the Commandments in Hebrew, on the fifth is the brass laver, and on the sixth is the Shulhan, the table, with the 12 loaves. Two cherub's wings, cut round, are attached to the narrower sides of the valance. The curtain is oblong and is lavishly decorated with a Hungarian motif, the so-called domestic embroidery. On each of its sides is a twisted pillar with grape and leaf garlands that stands on an arched base decorated with curved arcs and rosettes in the middle. Above each is a Renaissance vase with arched handle and tulip and rosette flower stems. On the lower part of the curtain, in the middle, are two curling garlands that rise out of flower stems and have pomegranates and tulips on them. The entire make-up is covered by the curving garlands that grow out of flower stems. In the upper part, surrounded by curling wavy forget-me-nots, is a rounded velvet inlay inscribed with four Hebrew lines containing the data of the donor. Inlaid in the middle is a heart and a closed crown. The material of the curtain is made up of four parts. Hungarian

1742 (according to the inscription in the inlay)

The valance is of the end of the 17th century

From the synagogue of Óbuda
Height: 230 cm.
Width: 148 cm.
Inventory No.: 64.1552

The valance's analogue: R. Roth: *Jewish Art*. No. 327.: Prague, 1764 (At present in the Jewish Museum in New York). It has a similar seven-part resolution.

For the curtain: *Judaica, Kölnisches Stadtmuseum*, 52. No. 10.: has the arrangement of five shields 36. No. 10.: the curtain of the Ark of the Torah of the early 18th century has similar twisted columns with Renaissance vase and flowers. R. Krüger: *Die Kunst der Synagoge*. Picture 34.: Torah mantle, 1697 (Prague, Jewish Museum, No. 12.669). It has similar twisted columns with grape garland.

Exhibited: Exhibition of Applied Art in Old Buda and Pest. No. 375

168 Curtain of the Ark of the Torah and Valance
(Plate IX)

The valance is brown damask brocaded with pink, beige and yellow threads (the pattern is made of a floating strip taken from a separate chest and does not run from one end to the other, only the extent of the pattern); has chemille edges and tassels. The material of the curtain which is decorated with gold braided inlays is the same as that of the valance. The center is an aquamarine satin with white strips of velvet woven into it, whose edges are corded silver lamé. In the center appliqué are also strips of blue-white brocaded silk edged in woven gold ribbons. The valance is straight on top and tasseled at the tip of its curves at the bottom. The ornamention is parallel rows of roses and forget-me-nots over a background of playing card patterns in its own color (hearts, diamonds, clubs). The curtain is oblong with the Hebrew inscription of the donor's data on two sides. The design has the look of lace and is woven in flowered and ribbed strips. The Hebrew letters signifying the Torah crown, worked in zigzag pattern material, are in the middle. On top is a bonneted crown decorated with dots. The material of the curtain is made up of two strips.

Around 1850. The middle part from around 1780
Height: 176 cm.
Width: 150 cm.
Inventory No.: 64.1427

170 Curtain of the Ark of the Torah

Green silk velvet. Decorated with couched raised embroidery stitched with green silk and metal thread. It has spangles, bells, red and green imitation gems. The curtain is oblong, its sides are rounded. Almost all of its extent is covered with late baroque and rococo pattern. There are ribboned lotus bunches in the corners. Four bouquets of daisies and palmettes issuing from cornucopias in the middle progress diagonally to the center. On the four sides, flower baskets of cornucopias on concave checkered base alternate with lily and palmette shrubs and patterns of tulips and bunched ribbons. Below, over the central bunched ribbon, is a flower basket with the flowers reaching upward. In the center is a cartouche with a rosette. It is framed in garlands and bunched ribbons. The four spaces left open in the middle have a number of lines in Hebrew containing the particulars of the donor. Above, between two prancing lions, is a small vase with dahlia, a closed crown over them, and the Hebrew initials for Torah Crown. The curtain is made up of three parts.
1772 (according to the inscription)
From the synagogue of Óbuda
Height: 242 cm.
Width: 164 cm.
Inventory No.: 64.1475
Exhibited: Exhibition of Applied Art in Old Buda and Pest. No. 277

169 Curtain of the Ark and Valance

The valance and the cover itself are dark blue velvet. The makeup is red velvet, gold embroidered applied work with red and green paste and rimmed with gold woven ribbon. The valance is oblong and has a flowing stripe on its two longer sides. The lower strip has pomegranates and six-pointed stars in rounded "waves", the upper strip has garlands. At the two narrower ends are six-pointed stars in a circle, a vase with torch, and a Hebrew inscription arranged in a semicircle. In the center, Mount Sinai in flames, two prancing deer above it holding the Tablets of the Ten Commandments, with five rows each of abbreviations of the Commandments in Hebrew. A closed crown on top. The curtain is oblong with rococo-style wavy garland frame. The makeup has a frame of curls and arches, the sides have stitched tulip motifs in the middle. There is a one-line Hebrew quotation in the middle, and at the bottom, "And you shall make an ark cover of pure gold" (Exodus 25:17). The makeup has an edge of thin line, on the two sides is a crowned prancing lion on a square-based Ionic column with diagonal leafed branch. They hold a closed crown. Three tasseled cords issue from the crown, between them is a tulip, the two Hebrew letters being the initials of "Torah Crown". Further down, between the columns, are three straight and two curved lines of Hebrew inscription, two hands in blessing and the Star of David. Two curving foliate motifs and three lines of Hebrew. The valance is made up of two parts, the curtain of four.
Made by Kálmán Grünwald
1852 (according to the inscription)
Height: 300 cm.
Width: 185 cm.
Inventory No.: 64.1532

171 Curtain of the Ark of the Torah (Plate X)

Tobacco-brown velvet attached to red velvet. Green and beige needlework, metal thread, couched embroidery and green flat embroidery, green velvet appliqués, spangle decorations. Trapezoid in shape, heavy baroque and rococo pattern embroidery. The top and the two sides have three-fold borders: between two narrow rows of leaves there is a floriate design. The tip of the upper border has two pomegranates, between them a half-diadem formed of curved leaves bending downward. At the two lower corners of the main body is a palmette and two curved acanthus leaves between them in the middle. Above those is a balustrated balcony with a ribbed vase at each end, one in the middle which has a bunch of roses. There are wavy flower garlands in the upper part. In the center, in tasseled drapery, are the two Tablets of the Law in a frame of oak leaves with the first words of the Ten Commandments in Hebrew. On the two tips of the drapery is a rose, above them a closed crown whose upper part is made up of petals and its bottom is decorated with tassels. The two lines of Hebrew with the details of the donor under the curtain are a separate piece attached to the velvet. The curtain dates from the middle of the 18th century, the attachment is of a later date.

Gift of Dr. László Salgó
Height: 66 cm.
Width: 65 cm.
Inventory No.: 82.1

172 Curtain of the Ark of the Torah

The frame is silver lampas with blue, red, green and yellow silk and silver thread brocade and launch (the pattern is created by a separate floating weave that runs from one end of the material to the other). The curtain center is tobacco-brown velvet sewn geometrically with metal thread and applied embroidery. It has red and yellow layers, green chenille, spangle and metal inlays. It is edged with woven gold ribbon. The shape is oblong, the edge covered evenly with

172

a bunched ribbon pattern of leaf, rose, and forget-me-not bouquets. There is an Ionic column on a square base with a rosette on both sides. A prancing lion on each as they hold a closed crown. At the bottom, between the two columns, are four lines of Hebrew with the donor's particulars between curving vines of laurel. In the center, in front of the tent-like tasseled drapery, bunched into three knots are the double tablets of the Ten Commandments with their five initial words in Hebrew.

1815 (according to the inscription). The material of the frame is from the late 18th century

Height : 166 cm.

Width : 174 cm.

Inventory No. : 64.1554

173 Curtain of the Ark of the Torah

The frame is red velvet with gold thread applied embroidery. The inside is green velvet with green silk thread flat embroidery. The shape of the curtain is oblong, the sides are curved. The five-piece frame is covered by a baroque pattern arranged in three strips. The curves of the two sides are followed by a border of tulips, rosettes and rosebuds. In the middle of the curves is a tulip, serrated leaves rise from it in two directions, and attached to them is a row of arabesque-framed tulips, forget-me-nots and rosettes. The inside border is a row of laurels and tulips. In the lower third of the middle section is appliqué in the form of rising steps. On it are four lines of Hebrew containing the donor's particulars. The frame is sewn together of seven pieces. At the two sides, the pattern is broken at the joints and is not finished at the bottom.

1818 (according to the attached inscription). The embroidery probably dates from the 18th century

Height : 206 cm.

Width : 133 cm.

Inventory No. : 64.1459

174 Curtain of the Ark of the Torah (Plate XI)

The curtain itself is silver rep, light blue with brocaded white silk and silver thread stitches, and applied and gold embroidery on the edges. It is decorated with spangle and green, yellow lamella. Between striped triangles forming oblongs are flowered shrubs in rhomboid fields surrounded by daisies. At the bottom of the inlay in the center

are two lines in Hebrew giving the particulars of the donor. Above them is a spangled stripe, on the two sides a Doric column with wavy curved pattern and on each is a prancing crowned lion. Between the two columns two deer face each other and there is an oleander shrub between them. In the center of the inlay, in front of a tent devised by fabric bunched together in three knots, are the tablets of the Ten Commandments with the ten lines of their first words in Hebrew. At the top is a closed crown with bunched ribbon. The curtain is made up of four pieces.

1826 (according to the inscription)

Height : 236 cm.

Width : 164 cm.

Inventory No. : 64.1463

175 Curtain of the Ark of the Torah (Plate XII)

The frame of the curtain is brown velvet. It has gilt silver and silver metal appliqué, gold woven fringes at the edges, and bells. The center is silver brocade launched and brocaded with green, beige, pink and silver thread. It is edged with woven gold ribbon. The curtain itself is oblong. On the two sides, beside the frame, are ten lines and above and below are eight lines giving the particulars of the donor in Hebrew. At the sides of the upper strip is a Renaissance ribbed vase with handle, and tulip, daisy and lily in it. There are serrated leaves, rose, peony, and daisy bouquets among the asymmetric stripes in the inlay. The frame is made up of four pieces, the makeup of six pieces. Polish

1830 (according to the inscription). The brocade of the inlay is of the 18th century

Height : 230 cm.

Width : 138 cm.

Inventory No. : 64.1551

Bibliography : IMIT 1915 catalog (No. 32)

176 Curtain of the Ark of the Torah

Yellowish white velvet, with applied and gold embroidery. Red and green imitation precious stones, spangle and pearl decorations. Oblong shape. The frame on the four sides has three stripes, the outer one being a smooth line, between the other two is a double curved intertwined garland with palmette design. Inside of the makeup of the curtain is a curved row of tulips and rosettes. The lines widen into a twisting garland in the corners. These point diagonally to the center. Tendrils, roses and vine fill the space between the garlands. Spread all over the surface are six-pointed stars. Two round intertwined curvy garlands, vine and roses on them, are in the center. They encircle two half-round and three straight lines containing the particulars of the donor. It has a six-pointed star and the Hebrew letters designating the Torah crown on top. It is made up of four pieces.

Pest, made by the firm of Károl Grünwaldt, artistic embroiderer, afte Ludwig Förster's designs.

1859 (according to the inscription).

Gift of Mór Engländer to the synagogue in Dohány utca

Height : 335 cm.

Width : 205 cm.

Inventory No. : 64.1544

177 Curtain of the Ark of the Torah

The frame of the curtain is butter-colored rep with interwoven flecks o its own color. Pink, green and silve threads are stitched into it. The edges are fringed cord and it also has tassels and bells. The center is yellowish brown velvet, it is framed with a gold woven ribbon, it has appliqué and is embroidered in flat and chain stitches. The entire curtain is oblong in shape and is decorated with zigzag patterned parallel vines with roses and forget-me-nots on them. The upper part is made like a valance and is edged with fringes. Over the center inlay is a row of tassels and bells. At the bottom center of the inlay is a washbowl and pitcher ; above them, three lines of Hebrew inscription containing the particulars of the donor. There is a zigzag column with piping on each side with a prancing lion on top. Between the columns and lions are the tablets of the Ten Commandments with their first words in Hebrew. Above the tablets, in a curved strip are Hebrew letters and above that are the Hebrew initials of the Torah crown between which is a form recalling an Ionic curve. The probable reason for this is that it is a stylized form of a crown. Two sprigs of lotus and leaves emerge from the middle of the double curve. The curtain is made up of nine pieces. The pattern is broken at the joints where they are sewn.

1843 (according to the inscription). The body of the curtain is from about 1770, probably French.

Height : 162 cm.

Width : 125 cm.

Inventory No. : 64.1528

176

178 Curtain of the Ark of the Torah
(Plate XIII)

The frame of the curtain is tobacco-brown velvet with woven cotton edge. The makeup is silk damask decorated with a geometric pattern woven into it in its own butter color. It is brocaded in light blue, green, blood-red, beige and silver thread.

The center is brown velvet with gold embroidery. It is oblong, its design is wavy stripes with a pattern of bunches of flowers. The upper part is fashioned like a valance and has one row of wavy arcs and another of fringes. On each of its sides is an Ionic column whose base is oblong and has a rhomboid in the middle.

On them are prancing lions holding a closed crown with a six-pointed star and the two Hebrew letters designating the Torah crown.

Between the columns are four lines of Hebrew inscription with the donor's particulars and in the middle, in front of a drapery arrangement held together in two bunched knots, are

the tablets of the Ten Commandments with their initial words in five
lines each of Hebrew letters. The
velvet frame and the brocade center
are made of five pieces.
1897 (according to the inscription).
The brocade material is from of
around 1760–1780
Height : 335 cm.
Width : 206 cm.
Inventory No.: 64.1527

179 Curtain of the Ark of the Torah

Yellow velvet. Green, beige and metal
thread, applied and gold embroidery
decorated with spangles and lamella.
Oblong. The sides are decorated with
an intertwining design of arabesque
border with rosettes. In the center are
seven lines in Hebrew giving the donor's particulars in an oval wreath of
laurels held together by a ribbon at
the bottom. Above that is a closed
crown with curving lilies. Two decorative ribbons hang from the crown
which is flanked by the Torah crown
letters.
1808 (according to the inscription).
From Nagykanizsa
Height : 120 cm.
Width : 86 cm.
Inventory No.: 64.1549

180 Torah Mantle

It has two parts. The upper part is
brown velvet with geometrically
stitched and applied metal-thread
embroidery and with red and green
imitation precious stones. The lower
part is butter-colored silk rep brocaded with green, brown, beige, red
and blue silk thread. It has a woven
gold ribbon border. It is lined in cali-
co. Oblong in shape, it has two sides
and both are worked the same way.
On the upper part are six lines in
Hebrew containing the donor's particulars. Under each of the lines is a
rosebud. Above the lines is a closed
crown. On the lower part are two
symmetrical wavy vines with bunched
ribbons, roses, forget-me-nots, ears
of wheat grapes and leaves.
Nyitra (according to tradition)
1845 (according to the inscription).
The design is from around 1750
Possibly Austrian
From the synagogue of Orczy-ház in
Pest
Height : 82 cm.
Width : 45 cm.
Inventory No.: 64.1543

181 Torah Mantle

Green velvet with geometrically stitched raised gold embroidery. Lined with beige linen. Oblong, with embroidery on both sides, but visible only on one, the other is worn altogether. The borders have a curly frame, the corners of which are developed palmette fashion. Two rounded and three straight lines give the names of the donors and the date of the mantle. On each of the two sides are three six-pointed stars. In the center, in the midst of stylized rays of the sun, are the tablets of the Ten Commandments with their first words in Hebrew. Above the sunrays are the two letters of the Torah crown with a closed crown.

1858 (according to the inscription)
From Pest
Height : 78 cm.
Width : 45 cm.
Inventory No. : 64.1447

182 Torah Mantle

Tobacco-brown velvet with green velvet appliqués, green silk and gold thread couched embroidery with spangle and bouillon decoration. Lined with beige linen. Oblong with two sides. On one side, in oval laurel frame, are seven Hebrew lines with the donor's particulars. Above them is a three-pronged open palmette crown with the two Hebrew letters of the Torah crown at its side. The other side is framed with a curved garland of grapes, leaves and tendrils. At the bottom are six lines of Hebrew about the occasion of the gift : "In memory of the dedication of the new house of prayer in the holy congregation of Pest in 1859. I hereby fulfill my pledge". On each of the two sides is an Ionic column on a base with a rosette in its middle. On each column, a prancing lion. Between the columns, stylized rays of the sun with a rosette in the center. Above the rays, one line of Hebrew, a six-pointed star and a five-pronged open crown with a Hebrew inscription on both sides.

Made for the synagogue in Dohány utca in memory of its dedication
1859 (according to the inscription)
Height : 81 cm.
Width : 47 cm.
Inventory No. : 64.1538

183 Torah Mantle

Green silk velvet. Green, mustard, red and blue silk thread stem and split-stitch flat embroidery, decorated with red and green imitation precious stones. Oblong. In each of the two lower corners is a bunch of naturalistic roses and forget-me-nots. Above them are three lines of Hebrew text with the donor's particulars. Above two rounded branches two monster figures hold the tablets of the Ten Commandments wih one letter for each commandment. On top of them, over a wavy ribbon with the Hebrew letters for Torah crown, is a closed crown.

Around 1870–1880
Height : 90 cm.
Width : 55 cm.
Inventory No. : 64.1553

181

Northern Hungary (?). The lace is from Upper Hungary
Early 18th century
The two pieces were attached at the beginning of the 20th century
Height: 58 cm.
Width: 87 cm.
Inventory No.: 64.1233
Analogue for the lace: Mária V. Ember: *Úrihímzés* [Domestic Embroidery]. Budapest, 1981. No. 130. Illustration 62

185 Seder Plate Cover
(Plate XIV/b)

White loosely woven cotton. Green, beige silk and gold thread embroidery, brass appliqué to decorate it. Oblong, the bottom trimmed, narrow geometrical border on the side, the top tipped, above a bent branch with serrated leaves, berries and little bunches of flowers. A striped fir cone in the middle.
Turkish or Balkans. Made up of two ends of a shawl
Second half of the 17th century
Height: 52 cm.
Width: 97.5 cm.
Inventory No.: 64.1231

184 Seder Plate Cover
(Plate XIV/a)

Linen. Red, blue, beige silk thread stem- and flat-embroidered with linen bobbin, lace edge. Oblong, made up of two parts. There are five rows of machine edgings in the middle. Narrow hem-stitching on top. The lower edge has tulips alternating on looped lace. The two oblong designs are framed in a domestic embroidered garland of pomegranate, palmette, tulip, and rosebud design. Above the picture on the right is a line of Hebrew inscription, "This valuable piece is the acquisition of Samuel Joel and his wife Jahet—God preserve her—the daughter of Abraham—of blessed memory." The picture is that of the festive Seder table with candles lit on it; there is a standing woman and a man in an armchair holding a cup. Around them and above them various objects—knife, fork, lamps, Matzah and rosettes filling up space. The picture on the left oblong is framed in a quotation from the Haggadah in Hebrew, inside are lamps, tankards, a vase with flowers, flowering tree, Matzah, knife, fork and rosettes filling up space.

186 Seder Plate Cover

Raw congress cloth. Mustard-yellow, brick-red, wine-red, beige, blue wool thread half cross-stitch embroidery with flat-stitch framing. Oblong. Hebrew inscription in a wide stripe border —quotations from the Haggadah. The makeup is framed in slanting arches with little space-filling triangles at the bottom. Facing each other in two corners are two naturalistic looking little perched birds, in the other two corners are two butterflies with spread wings. In the middle of one side is a man leaning on a cane, opposite is the figure of a woman. The center picture on the other side is so worn that it cannot be discerned.

Mid-19th century
Height: 53 cm.
Width: 54 cm.
Inventory No.: 64.1229

נידער מיט דער צארישער
קאנסטיטוציאן!

עס לעבע די דעמאקראטישע
רעפובליק!

187 Seder Plate Cover
(Plate XV)
Butter-colored silk. Mustard, green, light blue and violet silk thread stem, flat and knot stitched embroidery. Edged in gold fringe, lined with beige cotton, constructed of four parts creating three pockets for the three Matzot. Three U-shape handles on the lower side. On the top layer, in a circle, the instructions for the conduct of the Seder ceremony in Hebrew. Inside the Hebrew lettering, on the side of the handles, in a semicircle is a flowered vine with leaves, buds, forget-me-nots and roses, one end being held together with a ribbon. In the center, four lines in Hebrew and, above them, another one in semicircle.
Around 1880
Diameter: 40 cm.
Diameter of handle: 5 cm.
Inventory No.: 64.831

188 Flag
Red cotton. The text is hand-painted on both sides in white tempera. Oblong. Yiddish inscription in Hebrew letters. On one side, "Long Live Polish and Lithuanian Social Democracy", on the other side, "Down with the Tzarist Constitution! Long Live the Democratic Republic!"
Russia
1905
Height: 73 cm.
Width: 100 cm.
Inventory No.: 64.1105

189 Mizrah Tablet
Under glass in gilt frame with acanthus leaves and flowers in relief. Green velvet, applied with metal wire and red and green imitation precious stones. Painted paper, darker brown on beige in the center. On its edge is a woven gold ribbon. Oblong in shape. The velvet is almost completely covered by the rich pattern of the appliqué. A branch of roses, curved and thick with leaves, issues from the four corners. Curved ribbons go all around, bunched ribbons at the bottom and at the top. In the center, amidst forms of curved leaves, roses and daisies with open petals. The painted paper has a branch around it with berries and leaves and the word "Mizrah", Mount Sinai, a seven-branched Menorah and the double stone tablets of the Ten Commandments with their initial letters.
Around 1850
Height: 28 cm.
Width: 22 cm.
Inventory No.: 64.1224

190

190 Bonnet

Black silk. Its gold embroidery has a contour of cord. Spangled petal decorated. Triangular in shape. The part that goes over the forehead has a threefold border—roses between two rows of rhomboids. Above them, flower stems of pomegranates and tulips. A palmette motif by itself at the top.
Late 19th century
From Nyitra (worn by the mother-in-law at a wedding)
Height: 48 cm.
Width: 120 cm.
Inventory No.: 64.777
Analogue: Collection of textiles of the Hungarian National Museum (Inventory No.: 1961. 637)

191 "Jahrzeit" Tablet
(Plate XVI)

Beige perforated cardboard with blue, green, beige, red, gold bead embroidery. The frame is bound in brown velvet. Oblong in shape, but the two corners on top are covered by the frame. Edged by a thin line. At the bottom, "Preppare [sic] 1867 Leni Weidman". Seven lines of Hebrew text, the last of which, on the left, has a flower decoration, St. Andrew's crosses on the same side. A little bird on a twig, a palm tree and a rose in vase on top. The piece did not serve ritual purposes. "Jahrzeit" is the anniversary of the death of a member of a family, but the custom has not been to memorialize it with embroidery or other technique.

1867
Height: 15 cm.
Width: 15 cm.
Inventory No.: 64.1207

IX Curtain of the Ark of the Torah and Valance (Cat. No. 168)

X Curtain of the Ark of the Torah (Cat. No. 171)

XI Curtain of the Ark of the Torah (Cat. No. 174)

XII Curtain of the Ark of the Torah (Cat. No. 175)

XIII Curtain of the Ark of the Torah (Cat. No. 178)

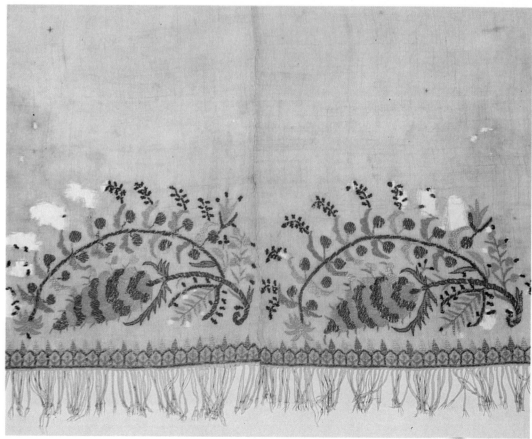

XV Seder Plate Cover (Cat. No. 187)

XIV/a Seder Plate Cover (Cat. No. 184)

XIV/b Seder Plate Cover (Cat. No. 185)

XVI "Jahrzeit" Tablet (Cat. No. 191)

ILLUSTRATED MANUSCRIPTS

According to our present sources, the art of Jewish book illustration in Hungary started in the first half of the 18th century.

Hayyim ben Asher Anshel lived in Köpcsény. The Köpcsény conscriptio (census) of 1725 lists him as scholae-rector, a teacher. The 1768 conscriptio calls him scriba comitatis, congregational clerk. In addition to these two occupations, between 1741 and 1782, he was busily engaged in copying books and illustrating them. He was moved by his artistic bent to do that, but possibly also by his desire to improve his finances. As of now, we know of 27 of his works. These are scattered all over the world's public and private collections. Dominant in his work is Hungarian, colorful flower decoration. His gravestone testifies that he died on April 20, 1784.

It was in 1777 that an anonymous copier and illustrator put together his Mohel Book with great artistry in Rohonc. The artist of the Haftorah Scroll, who copied and drew it in the same locality, is also unknown. The Sefirah Booklet, which is in the possession of the Musem of Applied Arts, was illustrated by Lazarus ben Yessaia in Németkeresztúr. He used rustic decoration, just like Hayyim in Köpcsény.

The 1792 Hevrah Book of Nagykanizsa, done by Yitzhak Eizik of Kabold is now in the Jewish Museum (No. 214). According to Ernő Naményi, his miniatures are "among the greatest creations of Jewish art".

Inventory No.: 64.633
Bibliography: Sándor Büchler: Libanon VII (1942) No. 3.65; Sándor [Alexander] Scheiber: Héber codexmaradványok magyarországi kötéstáblákban [Hebrew Codex Relics on Hungarian Book Covers]. Budapest, 1965. 187–188. 59

תפלה מכל שנה 193
Prayerbook for the Entire Year

Text: Prayers from the entire year and Sabbath, New Month, Pilgrimage Festivals, New Year and Yom Kippur and the Sayings of the Fathers. The illustrations: monochrome pen drawings. Title page: On top, a mounted man. In the middle, David with harp; on the left, Solomon with plumb line indicating building of the Sanctuary on the right.

2a: Shivity Leaf. Lion on top, Menorah made up of Hebrew letters in the middle.
49a: Cantor—with hand at his ear —at the pulpit.
70a: A man with Lulav, Succoth in the background.
73a: Cantor with a member of the choir (both have a hand to the ear).
76b: Sanctification of the New Moon (Kiddush Levanah).
Initials: 3a, 4a, 9a, 48a, 50b, 54b, 57b, 78a, 82b, 92b, 100a.
Moshe Leib ben Wolf (of Trebitsch) copied it for Yoseph ben Moshe Naftali Halevi.
1723
Gold engravings on 112 parchment pages
The Jewish Museum bought it with the assistance of the Joint Distribution Committee from the Königswarter family after 1945.
Height: 16 cm.
Width: 9.5 cm.
Inventory No.: 64.629

Bibliography: F. Landberger: "The Second Cincinnati Haggadah", HUCA [Hebrew Union College Annual]. XXXII/2 (1950–1951). 506–517; E. Naményi: "La miniature juive au XVIIᵉ et au XVIIIᵉ siècle. REJ [Revue des Études Juives] CXVI (1957). 59–60; C.Roth–B. Narkiss: Ha-Omanut ha-Yehudit. Ramat Gan, 1974. 125; M. Schmelzer: Scheiber Jubilee Volume. Budapest, 1984. No. 39

192 Book of Chronicles

Folio. Provided with Masorah (grammatical and textual comments of tradition). A single page of a three-column Bible codex. One column is cut off. The beginning of the text of the Book of Chronicles is an illustration made up of micro-graphic Hebrew letters: Eve holding palm leaves in front of her with one hand and passing an apple to Adam with the other. In the center is a tree with the serpent coiled on it. Probably, the codex had an illustration in front of every book of the Bible. From the way it is creased, it becomes obvious that it had been used for a cover of a book. The title on the spine is very faded and cannot be discerned. It is possible that it had come into the possession of the Festetics family with the "plunder of Buda" in 1686, the time of the reconquest of Buda from the Turks.
18th century
Square writing
Parchment
It came to the museum after 1945 from the Festetics Library in Keszthely
Height: 35.5 cm.
Width: 21.4 cm.

תפלה
מכל שנה ותפלות שבת
וראש חדש ושל ימים טובים
וימים נוראים ופרקי א
בות ושארי תפלות ש
וקדוש הלבנה · איך נתקן
החפורס"פ'ו המדינה כהרר
יוסף בכהרר משה כפתלי
הלוי" זקן
מעשה ידי משה לצהרד ושאף
ז"ל מטריכטש

במותיוק
אמשטרדם
תב"ג"ל

תפלה נאה לומ'...
קודם שנכנס לסוכה

יהי רצון מלפניך
יי אהי וא...
אבותי שתשרה
שכינתך בינינו
ותפרוס עלינו סוכת
שלומיך בזכות
מצוה סוכה שאנו
מקיימין ליחדא
שמא קבה ושכנתיה
בדחילו ורחימו
ליחדא שם י ה
בו ה, ביחודא שלים בשם כל ישראל
ולהקיף אותה מזיו כבודך הפדאש
והטהור נטוי על ראשיהב מלמעלה

194 Prayers for
Special Occasions

Text: Grace after meals, prayer on going to bed, sanctification of the New Moon, prayer on undertaking a journey, prayer at a funeral.
Illustrations: Red, black, green, brown colors.
Title page: Moses with the two tablets on the right, Aaron with the censer on the left.
3a: Two eagles holding a crown
4a: A family eating
5a: A man in toga kindling the Menorah

5b: Haman on the gallows
7b: Jerusalem of the future
11a: Gold initial in a blue cube
12a: The same
12b: Eagle
14b: Winged angel
19b: Kiddush Levanah (Sanctification of the New Moon)
22a: Basket of flowers
22b: Wayfarers
23b: Two ships
25a: Prayer in the tabernacle
26a: A basket of flowers
27b: Carrying a casket by people with Jew-hats

The name of the copier is absent
The name of the locality is not discernible
1739
29 pages of parchment
Yellow leather binding decorated in black. Of the period of the book
Source from which the Jewish Museum has obtained it unknown
Height: 9 cm.
Width: 6 cm.
Inventory No.: 64.618

195 סדר ברכת המזון
Grace After the Meal
(Plate XVII/a)

Text : Blessings connected with eating, prayers for women, ceremony of lighting Sabbath candles. Illustrations : Pink, blue, yellow and gold colors.

2b : Dedicatory page on green base with flowered frame containing gold paint

3a : Title page : Moses with his staff on the left, David with harp on the right. A Levite with pitcher between two angels on top : city panorama—apparently, Jerusalem of the future—at the bottom

5a : The family at meal

7a : The sons of Haman on the gallows, Jews in the foreground

7b : Judith with Holofernes' head ; a lit Menorah to the left

16b : A physician cupping a woman

17b : A burning of a piece of dough (Hallah)

18b : Woman in ritual bath (Mikvah)

21a : Prayer before going to sleep. Copied and illustrated by Meshullam Ziml of Polna (on the border of Czechoslovakia and Austria)

1750–1751

27 parchment pages

Yellow, gold decorated leather binding of the same period. According to the dedicatory page, it was given as a gift by Koppel ben Yirmiyah Broda to his bride, Gitl bat Savel Leitesdorfer.

Ernő Sós obtained it for the Jewish Museum in 1953

Height : 10.5 cm.

Width : 8 cm.

Inventory No. : 64.626

Bibliography : A. Scheiber : "An Illuminated Birkhat Ha-Mazon Manuscript

and its Copyist." SBB [Studies in Bibliography and Booklore] III (1958). 115–121 ; E. Roth : "Interessante hebräische Handschriften der Österreichischen Nationalbibliothek." *Biblos* VIII (1959). 83–88 ; A. Scheiber : "Ein in Vergessenheit geratenes illustriertes Büchlein der Meschullam Simel." *Biblos* XVIII (1969). 180–181 ; H. Peled—Carmeli : *Illustrated Haggadot of the Eighteenth Century.* Jerusalem, 1983. 31. No. 4 ; M. Schmelzer : *Scheiber Jubilee Volume.* No. 25.

196 סדר תפלת הדרך
Prayer on Undertaking a Journey
(Plate XVII/b)

Text : Prayers for a trip, Kiddush Levanah, etc. Illustrations : Colored. Title page : Ship with passengers on top ; people in the forest with canes and backpacks. Three words of the priestly blessing (Deuteronomy 6 : 24). Right and left a rabbit each.

3a : Precentor in front, father and son with the Succoth bouquet (Lulav and Etrog) behind him

4b : Kiddush at the table on New Year,

7a : Kiddush Levanah

11b : The attempted Sacrifice of Isaac (Akedah)

Copyist and illustrator unknown

1763

15 parchment and 4 paper sheets

Gold imprinted brown leather binding of the same period

Past owners : Hayyim Lazar Schwartz, Itzig Toch ; February 5, 1886, Emanuel Toch. Came to the Museum as Béla Dirsztay's gift.

Height : 11 cm.

Width : 8 cm.

Inventory No. : 64.628

Bibliography : About the Toch family : A. Marx : *Bibliographical Studies and Notes.* Ed. M. Schmelzer. New York, 1977. 330

196

190

197 Yom Kippur Katan Booklet

Text: Order of the service before sanctification of the New Moon
Illustrations:
Title page: Two recumbent angels on top. Moses with the two tablets centrally on the right; Aaron with the censer on the left
2a: Initial
The copyist's name is absent but, obviously, it is that of Samuel Dreznitz.
There is no sign of the locality where the writing was done. However, it is probably Nikolsburg.
1740
19 parchment sheets
Yellow, gold decorated leather binding of the period.
According to the notes in it, it came to be in the possession of the Epstein family. It came to the Jewish Museum in 1911.
Height: 15 cm.
Width: 10 cm.
Inventory No.: 64.631

Bibliography: A. Scheiber: *Aresheth* I (1958). 254–259; Same author: *Acta Orientalia Hungarica* XIII (1961). 135–145; Same author: *Aresheth* IV (1966). 490–592; *Grace after Meals and Other Benedictions*. Ed. R. Edelmann. Copenhagen, 1969; A. Scheiber: "Two Newly Found Works of Samuel Dreznitz." SBB [*Studies in Bibliography and Booklore*] IX (1969–1971). 33–40; *Grace after Meals*. Ed. I. Fishof. Copenhagen, 1983; A. Scheiber: SBB XV (1983).

תפלות יום כפור קטן 198
Yom Kippur Katan Booklet
Text: Liturgy before sanctification of
the New Moon.
Illustrations:
Title page: Text in colored frame of
flowers.
Unsigned, but the lettering and il-
lustration is the work of Hayyim ben
Asher Anshel of Köpcsény.
1761
18 parchment sheets
Contemporary yellow leather binding.
Both front and back, in the middle,
the *Tetragrammaton* in Hebrew. It
came to Samuel Kohn, Chief Rabbi of
Pest, from the Kohn family of Baja,
and from there to the Jewish Museum.
Height: 16 cm.
Width: 10.5 cm.

Inventory No.: 64.630
Bibliography: A. Scheiber: Yeda-Am
III (1955). 22. No. 8; Same author:
"The Jewish Artistic School of Kittsee."
Journal of Jewish Art VII (1980). 44–49;
H. Peled-Carmeli: *Illustrated Haggadot
of the Eighteenth Century*. 31. No. 5;
M. Schmelzer: *Scheiber Jubilee Vol-
ume*. No. 20.43

תפילות יום כפור קטן 199
Yom Kippur Katan Booklet
Text: Liturgy before sanctification of
the New Moon.
Illustrations:
Title page: Two lions on top. To the
right, Moses with the two tablets of
the Law, to the left, Aaron with the
censer in the middle. Below, two
eagles hold an emblem, in it—in-

scribed later—Sámuel (the name of
one of the owners).
3a: Initial
7a: Initial
8b: Two lions hold a wreath. A crown
above it.
Initial in the wreath
Copied by Tzvi Bonahers
Place where it was copied is unknown
1767
14 parchment sheets
Contemporary flowered yellow leather binding
It was in the possession of the Miser
family in 1888. Came to its present
place in 1917
Height: 12 cm.
Width: 9 cm.
Inventory No.: 64.620

זה השער
לה' צדיקים
יבאו בו ❖

דינים וסדר תפילות

יום כפור קטן

כתהלתי וכיירמי כתכלירת
ה'ומי כחמר עיניכם תחזנה
מישריס ככלף לבן וזדיו שחר
חני ה"ק והלבעיר כחלפי צראל
לכיב:כהרע סג"ל סופר סתס
נעשה בשנת תקכ"ז לפ"ק ❖

שמואל

זה השער
ליי צדיקים
יבאו בו

דיניס וסדר תפילות
יום כפור
קטן
כתבתי וכייורתי כתבלי
היופי על קלף נקן וכדין
טהורה כאשר עיניכם
תחזנה יושליס חניה״ק
והלעיד לסיבומהרטסג״נ
סופר

200 תפילות יום כפור קטן
Yom Kippur Katan Booklet
Text : Liturgy before sanctification of the New Moon.
Illustrations :
Title page : Two lions on top. At the right, Moses with the two tablets of the Law, left, Aaron with the censer in the middle. Below, an empty emblem between two tulips.
4a, 5b, 7b : Initials
Copied by Tzvi Bonahers Segal
Place where it was copied unknown
No date indicated, but is probably from 1767
Contemporary flowered yellow binding

Miksa Weisz bought it for the Jewish Museum from the Gestetner bequest in 1914
Height : 12 cm.
Width : 8.5 cm.
Inventory No. : 64.624

201 וזאת תורת הכהנים
Blessing of Cohanim (Priestly Blessing)
Text : Order of Cohen's blessing on the High Holy Days and Pilgrimage Festivals.
Illustrations : Drawings in ink
5a : The word *Baruh* (blessed) between two hands raised in priestly blessing
8a : The two tablets, Torah crown above them
11b : Picture of two fishes
Copied by Yohanan (of Óbuda)
Place where it was copied : Óbuda 1819
13 parchment sheets
Contemporary gold decorated brown leather binding
It was made for Zalman Kriszhaber (Bácskafeketehegy), an affluent and philantropic Jew in the County of Bácska ; his son, Simon Kohn donated it to the Jewish Museum in 1916
Height : 14 cm.
Width : 10 cm.
Inventory No. : 64.619

The date is not indicated. Made during the first quarter of the 18th century
Contemporary embossed brown leather binding
124 parchment sheets
Adolf Gestetner donated it to the Library of the National Rabbinical Seminary. From there, it was given for safe-keeping to the Jewish Museum.
Height : 12.5 cm.
Width : 8.5 cm.
Inventory No. : 64.622
Bibliography : See notes under No. 193

203 Copperplate Megillah
Text : Book of Esther.
Illustrations : Bibliography deals with them at length. Many examples of them are known (also at the Jewish Museum : Inventory Nos. : 64.2223 ; 64.2226)
Lettered, illustrated and engraved by Mordehai ben Yosl in Nyitra.
1834
11 paper columns
It came to its present location in 1915 as Lajos Steiner's gift
Height : 11 cm.
Width : 10 cm (of each column).
Inventory No. : 64.2228
Bibliography : E. Naményi : *Ein ungarisch-jüdischer Kupferstecher der Biedermeierzeit (Markus Donath)*. Jubilee Volume in Honor of Bernhard Heller. Budapest, 1941. 252–257 ; A. Scheiber : "Eine unbekannte Megilla von Markus Donath. *"Israelitisches Wochenblatt* LXVI (1966). No. 9 ; Same author : "Markus Donath's Second Mizrah-Plate." SBB X (1971–72). 80–82 ; M. Schmelzer : *Scheiber Jubilee Volume*. No. 11

202 סדר תקוני שבת
Book of Rituals for Sabbath
Text : This book of rituals follows the Cabbalistic orientation of Isaac Luria (Nusah Ari). It contains Zemirot (table songs) also Kiddush Levanah among others.
Illustrations : Monochrome
Title page : On the right, Moses with the two tablets ; on the left, Aaron with the censer. Two trumpeting angels hold a crown on top.
1b Crown between two angels
4b Initial
9a : The woman of the house lights candles on the table on Friday evening

9b : Cadet with lance in front of the enthroned Solomon
10a : Initial
21a : Kiddush at the Friday evening table
21b : Supper on Friday evening
36b : A family at the Friday evening table
53a : Havdalah (Ceremony of separating Sabbath from weekday)
56a : Jacob and his shepherd with the sheep
59b : Kiddush Levanah
Copied and illustrated by Moshe Leib ben Wolf of Trebitsch
Place where the work was done not indicated

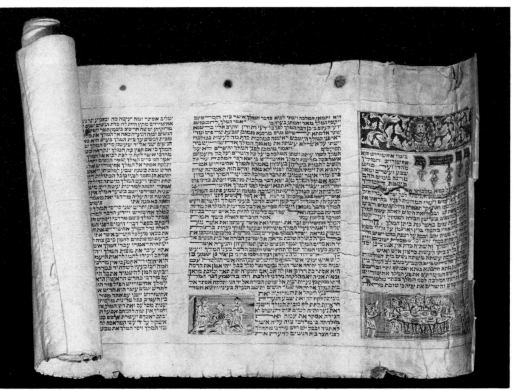

197

סדר הגדה של פסח 204
Haggadah
(Plate XVII/c)
Text: The text of the Haggadah with Yiddish instructions. "Addir Hu", "Ehad Mi Yodea" and "Had Gadya" translated into German.
Illustrations:
Title page: Two eagles on top. At right, Moses with his staff; at left, Aaron with the censer in the middle. A face on the two sides at the bottom
3a, 3b, 4a, 4b, 5a, 5b, 6b, 7b, 8a, 9a, 10a, 10b, 11b, 12a, 14a: Initials
12b: David with harp
The initials—with the exception of one—are interwoven with flowers colored red, yellow, blue, green, brown and gold. They have Hungarian character.
Hayyim ben Asher Anshel did the calligraphy and illustrations in Köpcsény.
1768

20 parchment sheets
Contemporary brown binding imprinted in gold
According to a note inside, it came from Pápa to the capital.
Given for safe-keeping at the Jewish Museum by the Fried family.
Height: 30 cm.
Width: 20 cm.
Inventory No.: 64.643
Bibliography: Fülöp Grünvald: "Kéziratos Haggada a XVIII. századból. A köpcsényi Chájjim ben Áser Ansel szépíró munkája" [Manuscript Haggadah of the 18th century. The work of the calligraphist Hayyim ben Asher Anshel of Köpcsény.] Új Élet X (1954). No. 4; A. Scheiber: Yeda-Am III (1955). 22—23

ספירת עמר 205
Omer Counting Booklet
Text: One day's counting of the Omer is on each page.

Illustration:
The title page is framed in gold.
Calligraphy by Hayyim ben Asher Anshel of Köpcsény (though not indicated)
1782
29 parchment sheets
Contemporary parchment binding with black decoration
Origin unknown
Height: 5.5 cm.
Width: 4.5 cm.
Inventory No.: 64.623
Bibliography: A. Scheiber: "The Jewish Artistic School of Kittsee." Journal of Jewish Art VII (1980). 47. No. 26

סדר ספירת העומר 206
Omer Counting Booklet
Text: The pages show each day separately as they are counted during the period of counting the Omer.
Illustrations:
4b: Seven-branched Menorah shaped of Biblical quotations
Jacob of Tiszolc is the calligraphist and illustrator
Place where it was done is not shown
1780
28 parchment sheets
Contemporary brown leather binding with silver filigree clasp and decoration
Was written for Yoseph ben Eliyahu Segal. Pages 28b and 29 contain notes by the Wahl family from 1822—1932. The booklet came to its present place in 1955 from the bequest of Dr. Antal Fuchs.
Height: 12 cm.
Width: 8.5 cm.
Inventory No.: 64.625

205

ד 4

אל מול פני המנורה יאירו שבעת הנרות

למז לחב נגי גן תמז מוזר שיר

ולאמים בארץ תנחם סלה

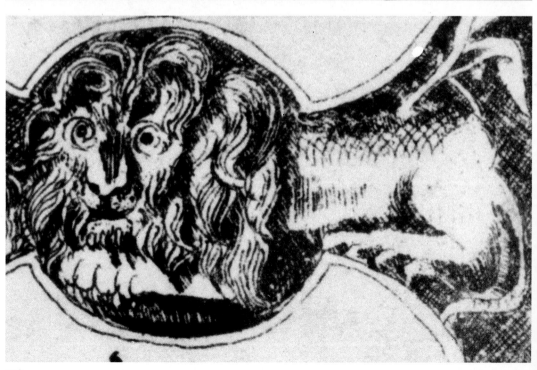

Detail of No. 207

207 ספירת העומר

Copperplate Omer Counting Booklet

Text: Order of counting Omer

Illustrations:

Title page: Aaron with censer at right, Moses with the stone tablets at left.

1b: Text of Song of Songs in micrographics

3b: Menorah shaped out of the text of Biblical verses

17a: Book of Ruth in micro-graphics. The rest of the pages are decorated with pictures of vegetation, animals and angels.

Written and engraved by Marcus Donath in Nyitra

1834

17 sheets of paper

Contemporary brown leather binding.

Originally, it belonged to Jákob Hirsch. Dr. Ödön Kálmán, rabbi in Jászberény, donated it to the Jewish

Museum in 1914.

Height: 10 cm.

Width: 6 cm.

Inventory No.: 64.627

Bibliography: E. Naményi: *Ein ungarisch-jüdischer Kupferstecher der Biedermeierzeit (Marcus Donath)*. Jubilee Volume in Honor of B. Heller. Budapest, 1941. 252–257; A. Scheiber: "Eine unbekannte Megilla von Markus Donath." *Israelitisches Wochenblatt* LXVI (1966). No. 9; Same author: "Eine Kindbett-Tafel." *Israelitisches Wochenblatt* LXXI (1971). No. 34; Same author: "Markus Donath's Second Mizrah-Plate." SBB X (1971–1972). 80–82; Same author: "Markus Donath's Mohel-Book." SBB XII. (1979). 9–15

208 סדר ספירת העמר

Omer Counting Booklet

Text: Rules and order of counting Omer. Each day has its page.

Illustrations:

Title page: Title of the book between two colored columns

Every page has monochrome initials drawn by pen

The copyist is unknown

Place where the booklet was copied is not indicated

The date (first half of the 19th century) is not indicated

32 parchment sheets

Contemporary brown leather binding, the spine has decoration impressed

It came to the Jewish Museum in 1918 as Gyula Pintér's (of Abony) gift.

Height: 6.5 cm.

Width: 5 cm.

Inventory No.: 64.624

209 Omer Counting Roll
Text: 49 cubes, one day in each.
Illustrations: Every medallion in a wreath of flowers
The copyist is unknown
Place where written not indicated
Date not indicated
Parchment
Source from where it came into the possession of the Jewish Museum unknown
Height: 8.5 cm.
Width: 5 cm (of each cube).
Inventory No.: 64.632

ספר הברית 210
Mohel Manual
Text: Order of circumcision and redemption (Pidyon) of a male child. Hebrew names in alphabetical order. Names of those circumcized from 1832.
Illustrations:
Title page: The text is framed in a multi-colored curtain. A crown on top
2a: Elijah's chair between two columns. Copied and illustrated for Moshe Flesch by Avraham ben David Beer

Sofer in Csab.
The book is from the early 19th century. The title page, however, is not dated.
Ten parchment and nine paper sheets
Contemporary red leather binding with the name of the first owner
Came to its present location in 1935
Height: 18 cm.
Width: 12 cm.
Inventory No.: 67.707

211 Ketuba (Marriage Contract)
Drawn up in Verona, the first day of the month of Kislev, 5441 (November 22, 1680). Marriage contract of Avraham ben Zalman and Leona bat Hayyim.

The frame around the text is provided by the zodiac.
Height: 72 cm.
Width: 52.5 cm.
Inventory No.: 64.1250
Bibliography: D. Davidovitch: *The*

Ketuba. Jewish Marriage Contracts through the Ages. Tel Aviv, 1968

XVII/a Grace After the Meal (Cat. No. 195)

XVII/b Prayer on Undertaking a Journey (Cat. No. 196)

XVII/c Haggadah (Cat. No. 204)

לתפעם רוחו ויתממר בריאותו ביד. חתנו אשישו ;

ונקרא תמזר ממר אהוא מאל זר ולמי הית עבירה ועני יצר הרע כן מוזך עלי הנבמה מהיכל זה וכל רואי הם יבחם
כי הם זרע פסול. ממר מאל זר וכל מעשי העשים עלי שהיא פסול ,מהיכל זה זלא רוח ה' זהוא תמונה כל כל מתם
הנבמות וזמו לסמני ו סימניך (יואל'ב'יט) את הלסוני דרחוק מעלכם וכנגד התיכל הזה בניתנם נקרא חרן תחפזרת
בהיכל הזה וקודה דק קורבה אל ספירות הקלי פות וממני יזלאים כל מתם רוחות הדקים המזוטטיס בעולם שהם
רואים ומרנים וראי עונברים לעצות נים ועני לפני דלה כי חלה הים עומרות דקלי פות העתינומית כב כאחרייס,
על אלו אלו מזונה ה' נסיר'א זמו והיא מלת חרמית וזל תמונה זהמו זהמנכה שהזה מזבד ה התילשות תטמאת ד'יתר ולהו
מורחים בזמיר ומחזיקים לבך שומחתם לעצוט ונים נסים בצעולם ל מתם בעד הקדוזים מן ההיכל הזה ה יצלא הם
חזק וזלוג וזריה מתחזיקים דלחן את הרזעים וזה"ה (תלי'סה' ט'י) תזלמן , ניר'כל היורד עומדים ד' פתוחים
בל רוחים וכלו חוינים ועמם מ ותים בפד הקדוזרה וזם מצעיר מוד הקד זה , והל מקום מתוקם לוהם יזי
תמות העולם צלת הרע ליזראל בצאת התיכל העמלביעית מבצ חון שה פתחי הם מלוונים כנבד הקדוזה ,ורם
מקמות לוה-לאבי מומרת העולם התסידיים צלה'הרבצא ל ליזראל ולא דחון חתם והגמ עלוהים רוה לוהם
שם כבוד צעל כן ומקיר לתם תור הקדזרה בתוך האפ-להה היה ועל זה נחמר (ישעיה ז' יט) מלי
גורלם סכנו בכדוד חי צני ורש צלה דחקו ליזרנהל ליזרהל ומראכי מלי-החי מגל-לם אוחיום ברהם דנים אותם
ג' סעמים בכל יום ברמחרי דדים הזיום בכל יום ,רום מעיניים על יזראל ועל אמונתם ע' ל
נבללות ענן הזיברות האבל חמנו העתקירעני מד ברי' זורד'(פקודי תרסה'ה) ולמחירת היה נרחלי
כי רום הנ בללות דוסף הקלישות חסר ממרנו בצער הקודה חמנו המסתבר כי הספי' הם נבללות בהכלות
ותהירוכלות והקברלות הבל ענן ח' וכנגד אבל הו'ים, והם סצעת מיני יצר הרע שהוא מקבל כח מאלבי תז'
ולכן נקרא צר ימרע בשבעה שמרת וחכי' הם' רע שחפה ,זונה ,חבן ,מבזול ,ערל, נפמי ,וכנגד חלה
ד' מדריריות בגיהנם שבהם מדן תחושא בן' מינים אלה :

צויר האבל באבילות שבעה וספר איוב ל פני וישב בזועפות פנים
יהי רצון שזה' בלע מות לנצח ומחה ה' דמעה מעל כל פנים '.

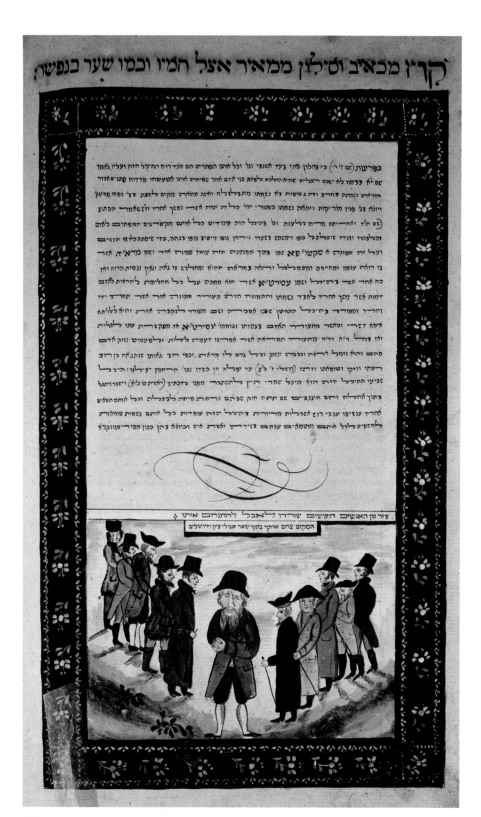

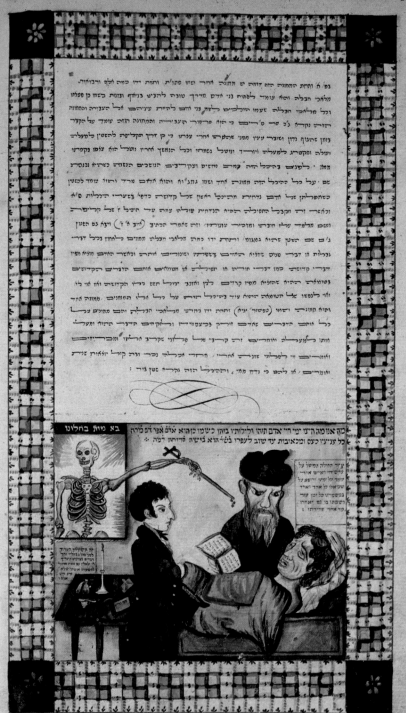

212 Ketuba
Drawn up in Rovigo, Tammuz 15, 5518 (July 21, 1758). Marriage contract of Sh'muel ben Mordecai Halevi and Esther bat Moshe Jehuda Sinai. Adam and Eve on top, a tree with the coiled serpent in the middle. The text is framed in the zodiac.
Height: 71 cm.
Width: 55 cm.
Inventory No.: 64.1248

213 Bikkur Holim Book of Nagykanizsa

Text: Instruction in Jewish literature on how to treat the sick. Prayers at the sick-bed, changing the sick person's name. Membership list of the society. Bylaws (Takkanot)

Illustration:

Title page: Drawing of a gate with text inside

Not indicated, but it is obvious that the artist wrote and illustrated this book in Nagykanizsa and is identical with Yitzhak Eizik of Kabold who did the Hevrah's book of Nagykanizsa (No. 214).

According to the testimony of the cover bound in silver, the book was begun in 1782. However, the first entry is of Tevet 10, 5562 (December 15, 1802).

Light blue leather binding with silver decoration. The four corners have square elements of decoration.

Two silver clasps

Height: 51 cm.

Width: 37 cm.

Inventory No.: 64.1075

214 Hevrah Book of Nagykanizsa (Plates XVIII–XIX–XX)

Text: Bylaws of the Hevrah (Takkanot). Cabalistically oriented texts. Selections from *Sefer Hassidim* [Book of the Pious], *Massehet Gehinnam* [Tractate of Gehenna], chapters from Yoseph Caro's *Shulhan Aruh* (codex) and Moshe Zacuto's *Tofte Aruh*, the description of hell's punishments

Entries start in 1769. Membership list and the names of donors to the cause of the Jewish hospital. There are last wills and testaments at the end of the book.

Illustrations:

Title page: Open Ark of the Torah The most important drawings deal with death, mourning and funerals.

1. Dying. A drop of poison off Death's sword into the patient's mouth. The physician is at the bed, around it are members of the Hevrah.

2. The dead person lying on the floor covered up. Beside him sits the person watching (Shomer).

3. Washing of the body. One of them holds a little fork (the dead person will use it at resurrection), the other one combs the beard. Three are praying. One has an alms box.

4. Carriage and two horses carry the body. Procession of people in street clothes and tall hats.

5. In the cemetery. The corpse is lowered into the ground without the coffin.

6. Cemetery with gravestones. Grave diggers.

7. The mourner passes through two rows of people. The sufferer's face is most expressive.

8. The mourner observes the Shivah (seven days of mourning). Book in his hand. Beside him, on a little table, remnants of the meal of consolation: bread, egg and wine. The mirror is covered.

9. The angel in charge of the souls of the nether world (Dumah).

10. Two angels raise the body and take it to judgment. Pictures of hell's punishment. Noteworthy are the two pictures of micrographics—Moses with the two tablets and the pitcher with the text of the *Hamesh Megillot* (Five Scrolls). There are also pictures of the chapel in the Nagykanizsa cemetery as well as its ritual objects—some of which are at the Jewish Museum. Calligraphy and illustration by Yitzhak Eizik of Kabold. Done in Nagykanizsa 1792

299 sheets of paper

Black leather binding with silver mountings. In the middle of the cover is the double tablet, embossed garland with flower decoration on its side. Engraved Hebrew inscription, "This book is the property of the Gemilut Hassidim Holy Society." On the four corners is a square embossed plate with Hebrew letters which show the date of 1793. It closes with a double clasp.

Height: 46 cm.

Width: 34 cm.

Inventory No.: 64.1067

Bibliography: E. Roth: *Yeda-Am* III (1955). 17–20; E. Naményi: REJ CXVI (1957). 71; A. Scheiber: *Die Anfänge der jüdischen Kunst in Burgenland. Gedenkbuch der untergegangenen Judengemeinde des Burgenlandes.* Ed. H. Gold. Tel Aviv, 1970. 121

215 Hevrah Book of Várpalota

Text: It appears from the notes that the Burial Society was founded in 1766.

Illustration:

Title page: Flanked by a lion on each side

The artist is unknown

Was started in 1822

Height: 28.5 cm.

Width: 24 cm.

Inventory No.: 64.1077

סדר הזכרות נשמות 216
Book of Memorials of Újlak

Text: Yizkor (May He Remember) prayer, Psalm 122. Mee Sheberah (He Who Blessed...) for the three Pilgrimage Festivals, Yom Kippur and Av ha Rahamim (Father of Mercy, a memorial prayer for the martyrs of the Crusades). The names of the departed, among them Löw Schwab, Chief Rabbi of Pest, and Raphael Goldberg, Chief Rabbi of Buda.

Illustrations:

Title page: Jacob on his deathbed. Kneeling on one side is Joseph in royal dress and shako, the eleven brothers on the other. Water-color. Genesis 49:33 in Hebrew.

Illustrated by Joh. Tallner "Mahler" in Újlak

1834

Seven sheets of paper

Contemporary, gold decorated black leather binding

It came to the Jewish Museum from the synagogue in Újlak.

Height: 27 cm.

Width: 20 cm.

Inventory No.: 64.1061

Detail of No. 216

וַיְכַל יַעֲקֹב לְצַוֺּת אֶת בָּנָיו

וַיֶּאֱסֹף רַגְלָיו אֶל הַמִּטָּה

וַיִּגְוַע וַיֵּאָסֶף אֶל עַמָּיו

Hevrah Book of Várpalota
Text : In it, regulations of 1785 (Tak kanot).
Illustration :
Title page : A tree in Paradise on each side, each has Eve with an apple Below right a lion, left, a deer
Made by Moshe Wolf Freudenberg in Várpalota
1837
Height : 37.5 cm.
Width : 27 cm.
Inventory No. : 64.1073

218 Hevrah Book of Jánosháza
Text : Membership roster
Illustration :
Title page : Bier followed by mourner being led by the widow.
Made by Feish Assod in Halas
Tevet 3, 5563 (December 28, 1802)
Height : 38.5 cm.
Width : 25 cm.
Inventory No. : 64.1072

Detail of No. 21

219 Memorial Page of the Hevrah in Gyöngyös

Text: Names of the officers of the Hevrah in rhyme.
Illustrations:
Scenes from the life of the Holy Society:
  1 Wife at her husband's sickbed
  2 Physician with patient
  3 The patient recovers
  4 The patient's confession
  5 Point of death
  6 The body is placed on the ground
  7 The appointee of the Hevrah sits up with the body and studies
  8 Washing of the body
  9 Placing the body into the coffin
10 The coffin is carried on shoulders
11 The body is lifted from the coffin
12 Interring
Below, forerunner of the Messiah riding a donkey, Shofar in hand.
Resurrection
Illustrator is unknown (the book was done in Gyöngyös)
1800
One sheet of parchment
Was donated by the Hevrah of Gyöngyös
Height: 62.5 cm.
Width: 60 cm.
Inventory No.: 64.1199

220 Shiviti Tablet

(used to stand in front of the cantor
Text: Psalms and *Hamesh Megillo* (Five Scrolls) in micrographic
Illustrations:
Jacob's dream, Solomon enthroned
Ruth, David with harp, Esther, once again Solomon. Menorah at bottom
Made by Mordecai ben Eliezer Cantor in Megyer
The New Moon of Adar, 588 (February 16, 1828) is the date of completion.
Height: 67 cm.
Width: 53.5 cm.
Inventory No.: 64.1240

221 Shiviti Tablet

Text: The usual formulas
Illustrations:
Torah crown on top. "S. D."—the
illustrator's initials—in two emblems.
In the middle, two lions hold the two
tablets of the Law. Two men in great
coat and stick in hand.

Hungarian style work
Made by Solomon Deutsch of Darás
Porpác.
Completed on August 30, 1869
Height: 47 cm.
Width: 42 cm.
Inventory No.: 64.1239

COLLECTION OF FINE ARTS

The collection of fine arts has not come about by purchases or because of a conscious decision of development. The fine art objects, by and large, came into the possession of the Museum as gifts or because they were deposited for safe-keeping. Many objects were donated by the artists themselves (or their widows). The Museum's first endeavor was not the collection of fine art. Plans for the long run called for only a small number of objects to be exhibited. Those were meant mainly to illustrate the rest of the material on exhibition.

226

222 *Wilhelm August Stryowski (1834–1917)*
Jewish Wedding
(Plate XXI)

Stryowski studied in Danzig. Later, he went also to Holland and Paris, then made trips to Poland and Galicia where he painted genre scenes. He was professor at the School of Arts in Essen from 1894. Many of his pictures are in museums. While this book was being worked at, the Museum was robbed of its best known work, the *Jewish Wedding*, painted in Poland. Figures in the picture are worked in great detail. The scene is somewhat theatrical: all this indicates a continuation of Munich Academism.

Oil on canvas. 105 × 195 cm.
No signature
Inventory No.: 64.1867

223 *Izsák Perlmutter (1866–1932)*
Woman Sewing
(Plate XII/a)

Perlmutter studied in Paris. He lived in Holland for a long time where he created fine realistic pictures and seascapes. On returning home, he turned to life in the village. In these pictures, the decorative character came to the fore which he treated impressionistically on his canvases.

The exhibited picture belongs to the artist's series of very successful genre paintings. The crowded peasant room is rendered in rich colors. The table, the cloth on it, the flowers and pictures on the wall, the beams of the ceiling all combine to create a decorative still-life as the background for the figure of the old peasant woman. Her looks reflect concentration as she arranges the creased fabric in her sewing machine. Her face radiates seren-

ity and simple wisdom. It conveys the good spirits of a woman satisfied with her lot.

Oil on canvas. 115 × 89 cm.
Signed at bottom right: "I. PERLMUTTER"
Inventory No.: 64.2307

224 *Adolf Fényes (1867–1945)*
Meal of the Poor
(Plate XXII/b)

Meal of the Poor is an outstanding example of the artist's *Poor Poeple* series done in Szolnok—which established his reputation. His puritanical style of telling the story is coupled with profound characterization. The young woman painted from the back has a yellow scarf on her shoulders, the white stripe of her apron in front is luminous. The man sits in a posture of fatigue. His face reflects the dull lethargic exhaustion of those who do heavy physical work. Above the table hangs a birdcage on the wall, under it a grater and a pitcher. On the ground is a jug and wine bottles in the corner, all making the genre painting into something like a still-life. Fényes arranges the area he paints purposefully, taking care that the essence—the figures—are in focus. With this painting, he succeeded in creating one of his best works.

Oil on canvas. 111 × 90 cm.
Signed bottom right: "FÉNYES A. 1906"
Inventory No.: 64.239
Reproduced: Anna Oelmacher: *Fényes*. Budapest, 1962. Illustration No. 18

220

225 *Adolf Fényes*
Moses Brings Forth Water
(Plate XXIII)

This painting belongs to Fényes's so-called "story period". It was done in the 1910s when the painter had already finished his *Poor People* series and was beyond his Szolnok period. Because of the threat of World War I, Fényes turned away from themes of daily life and drew his inspiration from the world of legends and fables. He aimed to give artistic illustration to stories in the Hebrew Bible, hoping to find there the solution to the problems that tortured him. This period of his life's work is less significant because of overdecoration of his paintings and their tendentious character.
Oil on canvas. 85 × 102 cm.
Signed bottom left: "Fényes A. 1914"
Inventory No.: 64.2340

226 *Fülöp László (1869–1937)*
Portrait of Nándor Katona

Fülöp László had been the pupil of Bertalan Székely and Károly Lotz, then continued with his studies in Munich. At first, he concentrated on genre painting, but soon he excelled in portraiture. The present portrait, comparatively poor in colors, neatly summarizes Fülöp László's virtues as a painter. The artist's paintings are characterized by their emphasis on the interdependence of character and intellect. He endeavors to show the most flattering qualities of his subjects. This is the key to his later success and his fame. (He immortalized many famous public figures; he had successful exhibitions abroad and

taught at the Royal Art School in London.) The subject of this portrait, the painter Nándor Katona (1864–1932), studied with László Mednyánszky whom he regarded as his master. His first successes were in the 1920s as a landscape painter.
Oil and chalk. 74 × 47 cm.
Signed bottom right: "To my friend Nándor with love
Vienna, 1902 I. László F."
Inventory No.: 64.2079

227 *Hugó Scheiber (1873–1950)*
Self-portrait

Scheiber's early works still carry the signs of impressionism and plein-air. Later, he developed his own individual style that was influenced by Weimar expressionism and the Futurist movement. There is much repetition among his pictures. However, with his best creations, he represents

the best in twentieth-century painting. He participated in Berlin in the *Sturm* Exhibition; his work was also shown in Italy and the USA.
Scheiber's self-portrait shown here combines the characteristics of his work: dynamic expressionism, cubistic disjointing of the elements of the face, grotesque emphasis, the fast and fevered beat of the composition. The lips are pressed together, the eyes look ahead in suggestive attention. The open neck of the shirt is drawn in lively curves.
Paper, chalk. 69 × 49 cm.
Signed bottom left: "Scheiber H."
Inventory No.: 64.2362

228 Béla Kádár (1877–1956)
Interior
(Plate XXIV)
At the beginning of his career, Kádár painted naturalistic pictures. In later life, the art of József Rippl-Rónai had great influence on him. In 1921, he exhibited in partnership with Hugó Scheiber. In the 1920s, he developed his own expressive-abstract style.
The painting shown, probably from the 1940s, represents his mature period. Characteristic of the painting are its rhythmic, melodious lines, the noble styling and surrealistic vision. The latter is common to all of the artist's last works. The nude silhouette is placed into the composition of objects around it that are only suggested. The vivid colors and graceful lines complement each other and create a harmonious effect.
Tempera, paper. 88 × 61 cm.
Signed bottom right : "KÁDÁR BÉLA"
Inventory No. : 64.2327

229 Vilmos Perlrott-Csaba
(1880–1955)
Still-life
(Plate XXV)
Perlrott was Matisse's pupil for many years. He began his career under the influence of Fauvism and Cubism. While he was traveling in Spain, he studied El Greco's work. This is evident in the structure of many of his paintings. This one reflects the elegance and decorativity he had learned from Matisse. Its use of space and coloring make it a truly genuine piece of art, and despite its dynamism, it creates a serene effect. The darker tone of the background emphasizes the decorative nature of the colorful bunch of flowers. Cézanne's discipline, present in Perlrott's other works, too, combines here with lyric ease.
Oil on wood. 68 × 48 cm.
No signature
Inventory No. : 65.1321

230 Vilmos Perlrott-Csaba
Immánuel Lőw on his Deathbed
This shocking piece of drawing differs form Perlrott's usual works in many ways. His aim in this is to be exact and authentic when informing of the fact of death and its finality. The artist wished to depict the lines of the agony of death on the face.
Perlrott underlines the tragedy of the event with his distribution of light and shadow and the emphasis of his stark lines. Immánuel Lőw, the world-renowned scholar, was deported from Szeged at the age of 90. The aged Chief Rabbi was taken off the cattle cars of transport in Budapest ; he died here. Alexander Scheiber had requested to have the face drawn in the morgue of the emergency hospital in Wesselényi utca.
Signed on the left: "Perlrott Csaba Vilmos 944 VII 20"
Pencil drawing on paper. 24.5 × 32.1 cm.
Inventory No. : 64.2087

230

231 *Ede Telcs (1872–1948)*
Portrait of József Kiss

Telcs was one of the most popular Hungarian sculptors of the late 19th and the beginning of the 20th centuries. At first, he drew his themes from the life of the people. Accommodating the period's taste, he achieved success with genre pieces and realistic sculptures. He had many government commissions and has a number of his creations gracing the public squares of Budapest. In addition, he also sculpted the busts of Kálmán Thaly, Miksa Falk, Puccini, Gyula Andrássy, Zsolt Beöthy and others.

In the bust of József Kiss, the poet (1843–1921), Telcs's lyric representation overshadows all naturalistic elements. The artist stresses his subject's sentimentality in the facial lines. The bust, instead of displaying the nervous and stern lines so often used by naturalism, radiates calm and serenity.

Bronze. Height: 57 cm.
No signature
Inventory No.: 64.2156

232 Béla Czóbel (1883–1976)
Young Girl
(Plate XXVI/a)

After starting his career in Nagybánya, Czóbel studied at the Julian Academy in Paris. Then he joined the Fauves. Later, Weimar Expressionism also influenced him. The themes of his lyric and richly colored compositions are the female body, landscapes, interiors, and still-lifes. These he varied, always from a different aspect, in sensitive and sultry presentation. The artist seldom tried to show his subject's individuality and character in an exact way. He regarded scale more important. He searched for the laws of proportion to be found in faces and bodies. He used colors to strengthen the feeling of form in his work. The loosely hanging red ribbon in the young girl's hair is used to create that feeling. There is strong cohesion in Czóbel's work, a sense of massiveness and finality, a sense that the picture could not have been conceived and painted in any other way.

Oil on canvas. 53 × 38 cm.
No signature
Inventory No.: 64.2057

233 Endre Bálint (1914–1986)
Woman Selling Flowers
(Plate XXVI/b)

Bálint was twenty when he first went to Paris. There he became acquainted with the works of Modigliani, Braque, Picasso and Matisse. His early creations are characterized by the impact of Fauvism. Later, he was inspired by Czóbel's post-impressionism and Vajda's constructive-surrealist painting. In 1946, he joined the European School of painters in Budapest.

From 1956 to 1962, he lived in Paris again.

In *Woman Selling Flowers* Fauvism is still perceptible, but the lyric sensibility so characteristic of Bálint and the attempt at simplicity of composition already come to the fore. There is a hint at the future artist with his unique use of colors, their free application into an artistic mass which is the sitting figure.

Oil on panel. 97.5 × 75 cm.
Signed bottom left: "Bálint 45"
Inventory No.: 64.2331

234 István Farkas (1887–1944)
A Memory of Balaton
(Plate XXVII)

Farkas studied in Nagybánya, Munich and Paris. Between 1932 and 1943, he exhibited his surrealistic, vision-like paintings many times.

In his *A Memory of Balaton*, the artist presents his main character, an enigmatic figure, in an imaginary landscape. Mountains can be seen in the distance. In the background, a walk along the lake, a statue on a pedestal, a bench, the fading silhouettes of chatting couples, and in the focus of the painting, a lone woman walking, her face clearly reminiscent of death. Farkas speaks of loneliness and dread and deep-seated pessimism. The coloring of his painting also transmits a feeling of anxiety.

Farkas takes advantage of his daring brushwork and ease that recall French post-expressionists to tell of his dread. The composition, created around 1930, is a fully matured result of this painter's art. It is one of his most important works.

Tempera on wood. 80 × 100 cm.

No signature
Inventory No.: 64.2341
Reproduced: Katalin S. Nagy: *Farkas István*. Budapest, 1979. Plate XXII.

235 Imre Ámos (1907–1944 or 1945): Tabernacles (Jew with Lulav and Etrog)
(Plate XXVIII)

Though the influence of the Nabis group can be found in Ámos's early works, it is interwoven with an individual, deeply lyric, sensitive mood and religious motifs. The colors accommodate their themes. The opalescent mother-of-pearl, the fine greys and browns melt into each other harmonically. During his 1937 sojourn in Paris, Ámos became acquainted with Chagall, who had a very deep influence on his art. His presentiment of the terrors of war and his own martyrdom inclined his paintings towards Expressionism, while he enriched his symbolism with motifs from the Hebrew Bible.

He created his *Tabernacles* painting in 1933. By that time, he had departed from the religious atmosphere in which his father and grandparents lived. The picture is of his grandfather as he observes the holiday of Tabernacles. He has a Lulav and Etrog in his hand, symbolic of the ancient procession in Jerusalem, as is the prayerbook with its Hebrew letters.

Oil on canvas. 80 × 60 cm.
Signed bottom left: "To Editor-in-Chief, Dr. József Patai as a sign of my sincere gratitude, Jan. 7, 1935. U. Á. I." Ámos Imre, 1933
Inventory No.: 64.2332

236 *István Örkényi Strasser*
(1911–1944)

Praying Youth

Örkényi Strasser's first exhibition was held at the Art Gallery in 1940. His better known genre statues are *Beggar Girl, Sick Girl, Mother and Child*. The artist often turned to the representation of Jewish past and present. His endeavor was—beyond spiritual identification—to give expression to eternal values. This endeavor is also applicable to his choice of subjects. His *Praying Youth* expresses the sincere experience of religious absorption, a constant theme in his work. Many of his creations were made in this spirit, especially the *Beggar Girl* and *Moses and Aaron*, in the Jewish Museum.

Plaster
Height: 43 cm.
No signature
Inventory No.: 64.2146

237

238

237 *Alfred Rothberger (turn of the century)*
Gustav Mahler Medal
Rothberger was active in Vienna at the end of the 19th century, and probably belonged to the Zumbisch circle. The medal shows the composer's profile. The inspired and purposeful face is romantically conceived. The dynamic lines of the wavy hair are balanced by the sharp line of the chin. The compressed lips stress the artist's ability to concentrate.
Bronze. Diameter : 50 mm.
Signed bottom right : "ALFRED ROTH-BERGER"
Inventory No. : 64.997

238 *Anton Scharff (1845–1903)*
Károly Goldmark Medal
Scharff was one of the 19th century's most important medal-making artists, who freed this form of art of conventionalism and rigid Academism. Also attached to his name are the planning and engraving of the Monarchy's coins.
This one-sided medal was made for the 70th anniversary of the birth of Hungarian composer Károly Goldmark (1830–1915). The exact, detailed work in the sharp and dynamic portrait shows off the thoroughness of Scharff's art. The details (hair, clothing) are in harmony with the essence of the lines in the face. The purposefully distributed play of light and shadow effectively underlines the character of the profile.
Bronze. Diameter : 56 mm.
Signed left bottom : "A. Scharff"
Inventory No. : 69.940

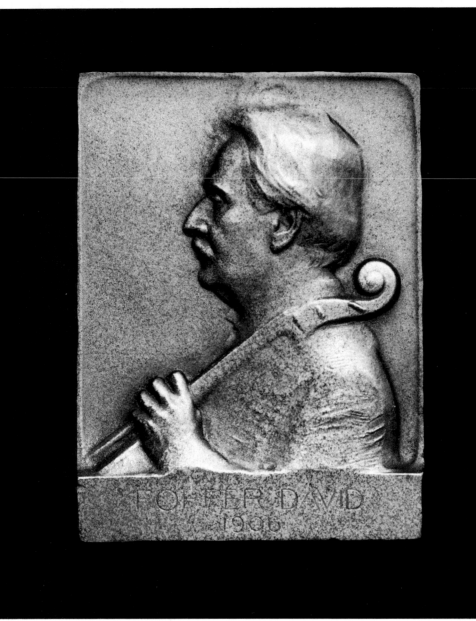

239 *Ede Telcs*
Dávid Popper Plaque

Telcs was a contemporary of Fülöp Ö. Beck and the generation of artists who paid attention to the art of medal-making in the early 1900s. Telcs stood out even among those with his talent for composition, his warm and intimate lyric tone, and masterly treatment of light and shade.

His plaque of the cellist Dávid Popper (1846–1913) underlines the truth of the above statement. Popper, who was the director of the Academy of Music's Cello Chair from 1886, was presented with this creation on his 60th birthday by his admirers. The plaque shows the artist's left profile as he clutches his instrument and is immersed in the performance of his music. The face of Telcs's subject also shows the feeling and spirituality inspired by music.

Bronze. 50 × 38 mm.
No signature
Inventory No.: 64.932

240 *Fülöp Ö. Beck (1973–1945)*
Ernő Naményi Medal

Fülöp Ö. Beck was one of the pre-eminent Hungarian 20th-century sculptors and artists of medal-making. He was going to be a gold-smith in Paris, but later continued his studies in the art of medals at the École des Beaux-Arts. His early work had a Secessionistic character; later, having been exposed to German influence, his interest turned to expressing himself in monumental form.

Ernő Naményi (1888–1958), writer in economics and art historian, used to be chief officer of the Hungarian Cultural Society. The medal, made in 1943, shows the profile of the industrious and versatile sage who for many years also served as the director of the Jewish Museum.

Bronze. Diameter: 60 mm.
Signed bottom left: "Beck Ö. Fülöp"
Inventory No.: 64.216

XXI Wilhelm August Stryowski (1834–1917): Jewish Wedding. (Cat. No. 222)

XXII/a Izsák Perlmutter (1866–1932): Woman Sewing (Cat. No. 223)

XXII/b Adolf Fényes (1867–1945): Meal of the Poor (Cat. No. 224)

XXIII Adolf Fényes: Moses Brings Forth Water (Cat. No. 225)

XXIV Béla Kádár (1877–1956): Interior (Cat. No. 228)

XXV Vilmos Perlrott-Csaba (1880–1955): Still-life (Cat. No. 229)

XXVI/b Endre Bálint (1914–1986): Woman
Selling Flowers (Cat. No. 233)

XXVII István Farkas (1887–1944): A Memory of Balaton (Cat. No. 234)

XXVIII Imre Ámos (1907–1944 or 1945): Tabernacles (Jew with Lulav and Etrog) (Cat. No. 235)

241 *Fülöp Ö. Beck*
Béla Lajta Medal

The Lajta medal, made in 1920, is a good example of Beck's talent for portraits. The sharp contours of the subject's profile are successfully softened by the distribution of light and shade, and are thus made rich in tone. The well-formed letters on the medal are also excellently distributed.

Béla Lajta (1873–1920) was the architect of many Jewish public buildings such as the asylum of the Hevrah Kaddishah in Pest, the morgue of the Jewish cemetery, etc.

Bronze. Diameter: 70 mm.
Initials at bottom center: "BÖF"
Inventory No.: 64. 898

242 *Aladár Gárdos (1878–1944)*
Mayer Kayserling Medal

Aladár Gárdos, sculptor and master of the art of medals, studied at the School of Applied Arts. Among his important works are the *Statue of Kossuth* in Sátoraljaújhely, the *László Paál Memorial Plaque* in Barbizon, the *Deák Statue* in Miskolc, and the *József Kiss Tombstone*.

Mayer Kayserling was a famous rabbi and historian. He had received his rabbinical training in Berlin and was rabbi in the Swiss Aargau in 1861. From 1870 on, he was the German-language preacher of the Dohány utca Temple. He lived in Budapest for 35 years, where he continued his scholarly work. The archaic lines of the almost Biblical face are made modern looking by the artist's use of spectacles. Gárdos stresses the severity of the bearded face, its deep seriousness—i. e., the sage's real nature.

Bronze. Diameter: 60 mm.
Initials left center: "GA"
Inventory No.: 64.934

243 *Gyula Murányi (1881–1920)*
Ignác Kúnos Plaque

Murányi had his training in Budapest, Vienna and Paris. Starting in 1896, he struck many memorial medals (Mihály Zichy, Beethoven, Haydn, Mikszáth, etc.). Many of his statues and medals are at the Hungarian National Gallery. Ignác Kúnos (1860–1945), the orientalist and university professor, received this plaque from the teaching staff when he was director of the institute, on occasion of the 20th anniversary of the founding of the Eastern Academy. Kúnos learned the Finno-Ugrian and Turkish-Tartar languages under the tutelage of Ármin Vámbéry and Budenz at the University of Budapest. Later, he taught Turkology at the same place as a *Privatdozent*. He traveled extensively in Turkey, Syria, Egypt and Asia Minor. He published many books about these places and his travels there.

At the upper part of the plaque is the savant's profile, and under the explanatory text is the Suleiman Mosque of Istanbul.

Bronze. 68 × 35 mm.
Signed left bottom: "MURÁN
Inventory No.: 64.931

244 István Csillag (1881–1968)
Fülöp Grünvald Medal

Csillag made this medal in 1957 in honor of Fülöp Grünvald's (1887–1964) 70th birthday. The subject was an outstanding 20th-century Hungarian Jewish scholar and an important educator. The medal emphasizes his striking profile. The high forehead, the line of the mouth and the deep-set eye all speak of a strong and concentrated intellect.

Bronze. Diameter: 96 mm.
Initials right center: "CS. I."
Inventory No.: 64.2642

245 István Csillag
Simon Hevesi Plaque

Csillag memorialized many famous personages of Hungarian public life (Frigyes Karinthy, Alajos Stróbl, Mihály Székely, etc.) in his medals. The creation of the memorial tablets of Attila József and Leó Frankel is also connected to his name.

Simon Hevesi (1868–1943), the poet and theologian, was trained at the National Rabbinical Seminary of Budapest and the University of Budapest. From 1927, he was rabbi of the Israelite Congregation of Pest, then its Chief Rabbi and the founder of OMIKE (National Hungarian Israelite Cultural Society). The Chief Rabbi is seen here in profile, rendered in a severe, puritanical style. The clerical garb is enhanced by the ripple of the cloth and the folds of the gown. The Chief Rabbi clutches the scholarly book *Reshit Hohmah* (The Beginning of Wisdom) in his right hand.

Bronze. Diameter: 60 mm.
Signed right center: "CSILLAG"
Inventory No.: 64.910

244

245

246 *Sándor Garam (1882–1944)*
Géza Ribáry Plaque

Sándor Garam was the student of Miklós Ligeti and later Béla Radnai. He exhibited often between 1913 and 1922. He settled in the USA after 1930. Géza Ribáry (1889–1942) was president of the National Hungarian Jewish Assistance Foundation. He fostered the National Hungarian Jewish Cultural Society's (OMIKE) development of theatrical culture by providing a stage for Jewish authors and artists suppressed by Fascism.

The medal shows Ribáry in profile in somewhat stiff and awkward contours. By deepening the lines of the profile, the artist has managed to emphasize his subject's ability to concentrate.

Bronze. 50 × 70 mm.
Signed top right: "GARAM"
Inventory No.: 64.920

247 *István Örkényi Strasser (1911–1944)*
Jacobus Mendel Medal

The artist made the Jacobus Mendel medal at special request. According to the text on the reverse of the medal, it was made "to commemorate the 1935 national convention of the Jewish Museum in Hungary". Jakab Mendel acquired great distinction in guarding Jewish interest as *praefectus Judaeorum*. The portrait is based on the seal of an old document.

Bronze. Diameter: 80 mm.
Signed right center: "ÖRKÉNYI
STRASSER"
Inventory No.: 64.902

248 Jenő Körmendy-Frim (1886–1959)
Ármin Vámbéry Plaque

Körmendy-Frim studied in Budapest
and Paris. The first showing of his
work took place in 1910 at the House
of Artists. Best known from his work
are his busts of Loránd Eötvös and
Ányos Jedlik, the statue of Frigyes Ko-
rányi, etc. He made many plaques.
Ármin Vámbéry (1832–1913), orientalist, university professor, was an
outstanding expert of Turkish philol-
ogy. In his many important works he
revealed the geography and ethno-
graphy of Central Asia and described
his travels. He was one of the founding members of the Hungarian Geo-
graphical Society. The plaque showing the savant's left profile was made
in honor of his 80th birthday in 1912.
The perceptive representation and
lyrical quality suggest a profound rela-
tionship between the sculptor and his
subject.
Bronze. 60 × 60 mm.
Signed top right: "KÖRMENDY-FRIM J."
Inventory No.: 64.927

249 Gyula Tóth (1893–1970)
József Joachim Medal

Gyula Tóth, goldsmith, sculptor, and
artist of medal-making, went to the
School of Applied Art and, for many
years, studied with Alajos Stróbl.
Later, he taught at the School of Applied Sketching in the capital. He participated in many exhibitions with his
medals both at home and abroad.
Notable among the latter were those
in Vienna, Munich and Italy.
József Joachim (1831–1907), composer, was a violin virtuoso of world
renown. The influence of Schumann
can be felt in his own works. His most
important creations were the Hamlet
Overture, Hebrew Melodies and Noc-
turne. The medal shows Joachim in
half-profile clutching his violin. The
artist fashioned the dress of his subject and the slight quiver of the
bearded face with great care.
Bronze. Diameter: 60 mm.
Signed left center: "TÓTH"
Inventory No.: 64.962

PLACE NAMES OF HISTORICAL HUNGARY

Bácskafeketehegy	Feketic (Yugoslavia)
Bácska	Bačka (Yugoslavia)
Kabold	Kobersdorf (Austria)
Kismarton	Eisenstadt (Austria)
Kolozsvár	Cluj-Napoca (Rumania)
Marosújvár	Uioara (Rumania)
Modor	Modra (Czechoslovakia)
Nagybánya	Baia Mare (Rumania)
Nagyszeben	Sibiu (Rumania)
Náznánfalva	Nasna (Rumania)
Németkeresztúr	Deutschkreutz (Austria)
Nyitra	Nitra (Czechoslovakia)
Polna	Polná (Czechoslovakia)
Pozsony	Bratislava (Czechoslovakia)
Pozsonyvártelek	(in Czechoslovakia)
Rohonc	Rechnitz (Austria)
Tiszolc	Tisovec (Czechoslovakia)
Újlak	Neustift (Austria)
Ungvár	Užhorod (U. S. S. R.)

Printed in Hungary, 1989
Kossuth Printing House, Budapest
CO 2724-h-8993